∞

CROSSING BRIDGES AND BURNING OTHERS

... A WOMAN'S JOURNEY THRU THE LABYRINTH OF LIFE

by Micala

∞

Crossing Bridges and Burning Others ... by Micala

THE THIRD OF A SERIES

(A continuation of the story begun in *"THE DAY AFTER YESTERDAY"* and *"FROM HERE TO ... EVERYWHERE"*, to be followed by *"IN SEARCH OF ME"*, the fourth and final book in the Crossover Series)

Crossing Bridges and Burning Others ... by Micala

ISBN# 978-0-9891072-5-9

To Jonathan with love and respect
for all the things you were;
with sadness and regret
for all the things I was not.
I have finally stopped running from life.

PREFACE

In my late 40's I hit a brick wall. All the role playing was over; all the deeply buried demons no longer tiptoed ... now they tap danced freely in my mind. I hit the bottom of a well and took a jackhammer with me to dig it even deeper. I deluded myself into thinking if I dug far enough emotionally, I would come out in a new place so much better than the one I had left. I never stopped to realize that even in a new place, I was dragging the same old me along ... warts and all.

... AN ILLUSION ...

CHAPTER 1

It was the beginning of autumn 2002 which didn't mean much in Florida except the summer tourist season ended with the beginning of school. Less traffic except for school buses twice a day.

I had the sense to know I was in a very fragile emotional state and decided to take life as it came at me ... hour by hour ... and do things on my own schedule. I slept when I wanted to, I ate when I wanted to, I dressed when I wanted to. I hated the doorbell and telephone ringing. I wanted no intrusions into my life and didn't want to deal with anything except the confines of my cocoon. I needed time and privacy to sort out events of the past and try to put them into perspective in such a way that I could go on. I knew this was a bridge I had to both cross and burn.

I returned to work within the general timetable I had told Carlo I would be back. It was a blessing in many ways, just as it had been when I first went to work for Carlo in 2001. There was just so much that temporary help can take care of, and the things that could wait on my return did. It was all I could do to keep on top of the daily work, and in addition try to chip away at the stack of 'leave for Micala to do'. Once again I hurled myself back into my professional life and felt like I could thrive on that alone. If not thrive, at least it would be a distraction until I could learn to know Micala for perhaps the first time in my life.

CHAPTER 2

My husband of thirty years, Jonathan, was totally out of my life. He had remarried six months after our divorce, and my companion of several years, Dean, was out of my life. We agreed it was the best thing for both of us.

Some time later, I knew it was time to take the next step, especially since Dean had gone back to Arizona and I felt free to come and go without the thought that he might be watching me. My life was very busy but very dull. I tried to bring a little entertainment back into my routine ... eating out (alone) ... going to a movie (alone) ... both of which Dean hated to do while we were together. I eventually ventured out to our dance club (alone) and was glad to meet old friends, but not glad to have to answer the same 'where is Dean' question over and over. My standard answer was 'we aren't together anymore' and I left it at that.

As time wore on, and in spite of vowing to never become emotionally involved with a man again, I knew what I missed was male companionship, plain and simple. How and where did I start. My parameters were very, very narrow. There was more of what I didn't want than what I did. Mostly, I wanted a male friend. No bars, no sex, no one-night-stands, no love, no marriage, no entanglement that would put me back on an emotional roller coaster ... none of the stuff that I knew would make me vulnerable again. I had never really dated in a normal way and didn't know how to do it now ... especially with standards 40 years behind the times.

I thought it through intellectually as I used to do with everything. Get some information. The internet was the source for everything else ... why not that? I found dating sites and after studying several, I reluctantly joined a few. Creating a profile was extremely hard ... I read what other women had put in theirs so I could convey the right message. Evidently my first profile sounded like one a nun would write, and the few responses I received were depressing but honest. Did I want to meet a man or not? What gives? Who are you kidding? Do you want a father or a boyfriend?

Message received ... grow up time. I took my first profile down and rewrote it ... I took the middle road ... safe but open to a new life and learning more. These responses were different ... evidently there were men out there looking for something similar, having been burned badly themselves. I found several wonderful pen pals. Safe enough for now ... at least I was beginning to rejoin the world, putting a few little pieces of a life together and I was doing it totally on my own. Then Dean called.

CHAPTER 3

We had a polite conversation ... not sure the reason he called ... was it to take my emotional temperature or find out if I had second thoughts about being on my own? There was a hidden agenda to be sure. I nervously ended the call and sat back in my recliner. It started again ... the shaking ... the sobbing ... hard to breathe ... memories flashing through my mind, unconnected, disjointed. I nearly jumped out of my chair when the phone rang again. It was Veronica.

As soon as I answered she knew I was having another panic attack. I told her about Dean's call ... that must have been the trigger but I had been nervous all day. We talked a long time about everything and nothing and I could feel the calm return. (Did I have epilepsy? Was I having seizures?) Fritz had his final walk, I went to bed and fell into exhausted slumber immediately.

... LOOKING FOR LOVE IN ALL THE PLACES ...
CHAPTER 4

The weeks that followed fell into a very structured routine with one exception ... I had become very active on the dating site, writing to many men and under the strict guidelines of internet dating, actually began to go out with several of them. It became more exciting than scary once I learned the drill. Actually it was a very safe way to meet people. We emailed anonymously until we felt comfortable enough to exchange names and phone numbers, then we spoke on the phone, and by the first date we had already crossed the line of awkwardness.

I had the additional advantage of having access to several legal sites where I could check on backgrounds, court records and arrest records. Before I met anyone for lunch (the suggested meal ... during daylight, public place, meet there instead of him picking you up), I felt fairly confident I knew a lot more about them than they did about me. I didn't encounter many surprises ... if I did, they were pleasant. The most difficult part of this procedure was when, having spent so much time making an emotional investment in the preliminary, one or the other of us would realize it just wasn't right for us to pursue a friendship once we met. Ouch. There is just so much you can know without actually meeting. Chemistry I think it is called.

Rarely was I the one to do the rejecting since any man I finally met had already passed muster. When I was the one being rejected ... it usually came in the form of no more emails or phone calls and it was a devastating blow. Far beyond what it should have been in this game of chance and I would usually end up having one of the panic attacks.

Call Veronica ... talk to her ... I didn't want to do it but it was the only way I knew to work thru it. She was a fairly recent newlywed herself (2nd marriage), taught school part time and I really hated taking her time. Angel that she was and is, she berated me harshly every time I started a conversation with "I'm sorry to bother you." We would talk it out ... mostly I talked and she listened ... and after awhile of verbal dumping, I was able to calm down enough to return to reality. I was always exhausted after an attack ran its course, and I usually went to bed or sleep soon after we talked.

CHAPTER 5

Walter was the first real pen pal I had online. His profile was striking and we seemed to match almost too well. His picture reminded me of Clark Gable and his writing skills were beyond anyone I ever communicated with before or since. I learned he wanted absolutely nothing more than someone to talk to. That was OK with me for a long time, but after months of writing every day ... sometimes more than once, eventually I became weary of trying to help solve his problems. I was trying to live for the future and he was living in the past.

His wife had died a tragic death after a prolonged illness and he had moved 3,000 miles to escape the memories. We lived 70 miles apart and that was the reason he gave that we couldn't date. The real reason was he was pretending he had rejoined the living but couldn't bear to be around another woman. He finally told me he had tried a few casual dates in his area, but he wasn't ready. I had fallen in love with a man I never met and when the futility of the situation finally sank in, Veronica was there to catch me when I fell into several repeated attacks. I wanted so much to just meet him and felt a tremendous sense of rejection and abandonment when he made no effort to meet me. At one point, I was tempted to drive the 70 miles and go past his house, hoping he would be working in his beloved garden so I could just see him.

Walter and I spoke on the telephone a few times but eventually our emails became less frequent, and one day I noticed I hadn't heard from him for several weeks. I never heard from him again. I didn't try to contact him again either. I felt a sense of sadness, rejection and abandonment all at once, but enough of my rational thinking was still intact to know it would have never worked between us ... the ghosts in his life would forever be in whatever relationship he had and I didn't want or need that in my life.

Then and there I decided that I would never be involved with a widowed man again. I could never compete with or compare to someone else's memories. Better to take my chances with someone who had been divorced ... I stood a better chance against a bad ex-wife.

CHAPTER 6

A younger (by fourteen days) brother. A divorced father of five, Drew was a ruggedly handsome man I met on the internet too. He was a New England transplant to Florida, living about twenty miles away taking care of his aging parents. In spite of that limitation, we wrote to each other often and I felt a deep kinship with him.

At our first meeting ... breakfast in a restaurant ... I was surprised by what a striking man he was ... tall, heavyset, white beard, well dressed and well spoken. He could have easily won a Hemingway look alike contest. We quickly moved beyond the small talk and were eager to know about each other's lives. We had learned a lot thru writing, but a real conversation was different.

We each revealed our tortured pasts a step at a time, testing the other's tolerance rate as we went. An only child, his parents had regrettably interrupted his life a few years before and asked him to take over when they could no longer manage on their own. They had no one else to turn to. Both in their '80s, his father was blind and his mother was doing battle with her own health problems. Because of this, he said, he had limited opportunities for dating, but really needed friends to maintain his own sanity.

I came to learn that his sanity was as fragile as mine, or more so. He was bi-polar and also suffered from clinical depression, both kept under control with medication. He was also a recovering alcoholic, having been clean for many years. Thanks, he said, to a strong belief in God and the intervention of some special people.

The love of his life ... his one and only wife ... was still living and still had a special place in his heart. They had married young, had their children, and he was a successful business man. He thought it would last forever. It didn't. After a few years her mind began to take her to odd and unpredictable places. She became very unstable and he had to assume more of the parenting role, along with being the sole financial support for the seven of them.

Within a few years, she finally moved into an area he couldn't reach. She was hospitalized and diagnosed with multiple personality disorder. Her doctors told Drew it was unlikely she could ever assimilate into normal society again.

He started drinking heavily, all the while trying to keep his family together and keep his business going. He suffered alone, not wanting his children further traumatized by his undoing. Friends and family were able to offer only limited help. The weight of carrying such a heavy load took him down. The depression set in and the pain was unbearable.

Having lost all perspective and rational thinking, he tried to commit suicide on the darkest day of his life.

Drew was hospitalized for a long time. With extensive analysis and medication, he was finally able to become an outpatient and slowly rebuild his life. His long struggle had taken a wretched toll on his life. His children were by then on their own, his former wife (whom he had been advised to divorce for financial reasons) was in her own world behind guarded gates, his business was gone along with most of his assets. He was declared medically disabled and would never work again.

During the few years he had before being called on by his parents to become a care giver once again, he was able to cobble together a very low key existence to accommodate his own limitations. Friends, family, church life and AA meetings became his support system from then on. Freed of the obligations of raising children and unsuccessful efforts to help his crippled wife, Drew began again and lived one day at a time.

I had met someone in worse shape than I was emotionally, although he was determined to live in spite of it. Part of his recovery process was acknowledging his demons and facing them square on. He knew he couldn't add any more to his life than he had at the time we met. That included serious involvement with another woman or marriage. He was much wiser than I was in that department, but that became the basis for our friendship. I never allowed myself to fall in love with Drew, but I came to love him in a different way. We trusted each other completely. We knew our darkest secrets were safe with each other. We had a common bond with our mutual emotional frailties that few others could understand. We could call ... and did ... at any hour to reach out for comfort and understanding. Without the pressure of playing the dating game, Drew became the brother I never had and I became the sister he never had.

CHAPTER 7

The first pen pal I actually became close to was Frank. He lived about 200 miles away and we knew we could just be friends. He was near retirement for health reasons and had a very sad past. He had lost two wives ... one to a tornado injury and one to cancer ... and was not looking for another one. He did admit to being terribly lonely as I was. He came to see me one weekend. He stayed at a motel ... I wasn't ready and didn't think I would ever be ready for that part of the equation in a casual relationship. He was also too much of a gentleman to expect anything else.

He was an uncut diamond but my attraction to his quiet, calm, gentle ways was immediate. It was a wonderful weekend ... his old fashioned or little boy ways of holding hands ... stealing a kiss on the cheek ... were so sweet that I was completely taken in by his charm.

The mechanics couldn't have been more different ... our lifestyles, our backgrounds, habits, routines ... but that didn't matter at the time. I began to play the mental game of who could move to be closer ... actually neither of us could or should ... we both had deep roots where we lived. All the same, wasn't it what we felt that counted the most? Sure, but it had to work day-to-day as well. I couldn't imagine myself joining his lifestyle and I am sure he felt the same about mine. I said I never wanted to get married again but here I was starting to figure out a way that Frank and I could do just that.

This mental pattern would become a habit with other men that I found impossible to break. Same loop every time over and over. Didn't other women mentally couple their first name to his last to see how it sounded? Did other people do this mental footwork so early in a relationship or was I a sick puppy?

Frank and I had a tearful departure that first weekend, with kisses and promises we would do this again soon. I watched him drive away and cried as I walked back inside and the rest of Sunday evening. I didn't know why ... I just did.

"Hello Veronica" ... she expected my call since she knew about my weekend plans. As usual, I was drained after we talked, and especially after such an emotional weekend. I took comfort in the thought that I would be back to my structured life the next day at work. At the same time, I hated the idea.

CHAPTER 8

Enter Edward ... finally someone in my city. We emailed several times but he preferred talking on the phone. Perhaps one reason were his verbal skills and deep intoxicating voice that could seduce almost any woman sight unseen. I was on guard for this one ... so far I had not encountered a real 'lady's man' but thought I would know one when I saw ... or heard ... one. I knew I never wanted to be part of someone's harem. Even so, I agreed to meet for dinner one evening and when I drove in I caught a glimpse of him. He was leaning against a tall flower urn, smoking a cigarette, silk shirt open to reveal a large gold necklace, tanned, and thick silver hair ... just a little longer than usually seen on men of his age, but very becoming. I parked and as I walked up to meet him, I couldn't believe what I saw.

I could just tell that Edward was one of those men mama warns us about. A showman. The chemistry between us was immediate. Being armed and guarded against this, I decided to play along for the fun of it. If what came out of his mouth was anything close to what I saw, this should be quite an evening. It was and more so. The word eloquent was invented for him; his self assured posture; his wide smile; his impeccable manners; the 'reserved' table he escorted me to let me know he was a man of the world ... his world but not the one I was in. He ordered every course for us, chose drinks, entrees, dessert, cordials ... we danced ... we ate (he ordered escargot as an appetizer and I ate it with gusto as though I had it every night of the week ... I couldn't believe I would ever even taste a snail much less eat one).

We talked for hours after the two hour meal ... the owner had to politely tell us he was about to close near midnight and that was our cue to leave. Only then did I notice the restaurant was empty except for us. He walked me to my car, but we couldn't stop talking. No subject was beyond his reach; no subject too mundane or too complex. We kissed goodnight and when he said he wanted to see me again I thought I would faint with astonishment.

I couldn't help myself. I was under his spell in spite of my own guard rails. I was also bewildered why he would want to see me again ... surely he could be out with any woman in town ... much younger, prettier ... he was at first glance the type of man you would expect to see escorting 'eye candy'. I drove home in a stupor ... it was too late to call Veronica but she had left several emails wanting to know what happened that evening. What could I say? I didn't even know myself. I sent her a late night email that said something to the effect of 'Wow' and left it at that.

Crossing Bridges and Burning Others ... by Micala

My feet didn't touch the ground for days. I had met someone who completely sweeps a woman off her feet without her even being aware of it, or being aware of it but doesn't care that it is part of a very calculated ancient ritual. I couldn't fault him for a thing ... I could have stopped the dance at any point but didn't really want to.

He called ... again and again ... and we went out ... again and again ... and I fell in love ... again. He was the most passionate and intense and self assured person I had ever known in my life. He was also very intelligent and a Humphrey Bogart remake in looks, charm, charisma, that certain *something* that just lights up a room. He had what they call style.

There was more to Edward than I knew then ... there had to be to bring him to this point in his life. His patina had come from many years of polishing. I felt ill equipped to pursue a future with him, but at the same time had a burning desire to know more about him. He was different.

CHAPTER 9

The married man ... ah yes, the one-who-has-a-terrible-wife-and-is-so unhappy-and-could-we-just-be-friends man. (As a very wise person once told me, there is a snake under every rock if you turn it over.) Eric had a hidden profile on the dating site, but saw mine and emailed me first. He had his profile down to edit it. (RED FLAG I didn't see.) We emailed several times, talked on the phone, and if what he said was true, was definitely someone who could be on the 'A' list.

A retired executive from one of the biggest companies in the country doing government contract work, his stories told me what a man of the world he was ... the whole world.

Having recently moved to Florida from California and unfamiliar with the area, we met in a parking lot and I led him to the restaurant he had asked me to suggest for lunch. When I pulled up alongside him, I got out to see an elegant man waiting beside an elegant car. If ever a man could be called beautiful, he was. Tall, slim, pure white hair, perfectly groomed, well dressed, complete finesse, total class. As I drove the several miles to the restaurant I thought what a waste of time this was ... it ain't gonna work. Small town girl born in the coal fields meets someone like him.

The package was perfect and I could tell it was from having lived a lifelong lifestyle so unlike mine that it would be best just to get the meal over with and move on. I didn't want to embarrass myself or him either, although we had talked a lot before we met and surely he knew I didn't match him in class. I had manners, could hold a decent conversation, knew which fork to use and which glass held what beverage, but Eric was far beyond that. He was definitely in the upper part of the upper class.

Sometime during the meal and the small talk I casually asked if he was divorced or widowed. I had assumed he was single since he contacted me from a dating site and I hadn't seen his profile.

"Neither." I looked up and asked what he meant. He was still married but separated *most of the time* and would be filing for a divorce soon. (BIG RED FLAG) Oh crap ... why didn't I see this one coming. Of course his profile was down for editing ... so he wouldn't be seen and could contact whomever he wanted.

I was not going to reduce my standards of being a lady by jumping up and storming out of the restaurant. I finished my meal and made even smaller talk than before. He wasn't completely satisfied with his meal and said next time he would like to go somewhere nice. This was one of the nicest restaurants in town ... I couldn't imagine what he was used to. I politely told him there would not be a next time since he was married.

"Could we just be friends? Could we at least keep in touch by email until this ordeal is over and I will be free to see you?"

Against everything in my mind that said NO, my heart said yes. I felt sorry for him (EVEN BIGGER RED FLAG). If he needed someone to talk to, I guess I could be that person. I could also help give him directions to places he was still unfamiliar with and suggest doctors, pharmacies, etc.... I told him I wouldn't see him again socially until, if or when, he was single. Some people know a dumb blonde when they see one. He did and I was. Well, not dumb ... just naive and inexperienced ... and the blonde part came from a bottle to cover my grey hair ... it had for years.

He appeared at my work place a week or so later and told Carlo he was taking me to lunch. It would have been an awkward refusal, so I went. He apologized for getting off on the wrong foot and promised his intentions were honorable. His behavior backed him up ... that day.

CHAPTER 10

Drew, Walter, Frank, Edward, Eric and several others were all in my life at the same time. Calling, emails, instant message on the computer, dating, I hardly knew how to keep it all under control. I admitted only to myself that I was having a thrilling experience. Men ... more than one ... vying for my attention. Some of the 'others' were single dates only ... several were pond scum once I got to know them ... some remained pen pals for a very long time .

One (a stock broker) fancied himself a Romeo and computer whiz who loved the balancing act. Sweet talking words that would melt steel. Type A personality. We chatted by instant message a lot but never met. The balancing act misfired one evening when he sent me an instant message he intended for a guy friend he was also messaging with. It said 'wish me luck ... hot date tonight ... hope to score big time'. When we both realized what had happened, he sent me a message that just said 'oops sorry'.

He immediately went into the 'block' mode on my computer and rather than let it lead to an abandonment episode, I laughed so hard I cried. Slick jock hoisting himself on his own petard ... the thought of it gave me a rush ... finally one of these jerks getting theirs and I was there when it happened.

My entire life revolved around a new routine repeated day after day. Get up, walk Fritz, get ready, go to work, walk Fritz at lunch, eat, back to work, rush home, pick up the mail, walk Fritz, grab something I could eat at the computer, get online and start the evening. Read emails, answer emails, chat through instant message (often 2 or 3 at a time), talk on the phone, go to the dating sites, continue this routine until I was so exhausted I had to go to bed.

Weekends I was up early to do laundry, cleaning, process the week's mail, grocery shop, banking, errands ... as fast as I could so I could spend time getting ready for a date or dates. Sunday was kept clear for dates and more computer time. I had to keep it all on a calendar. I talked to Veronica every night and gave her an update. I always wanted to know about her life, but she would laugh and say compared to mine, hers was dull. I saved my other calls for Sunday ... Mother, my other sisters ... Celeste, other friends.

The rush of this heady experience lasted several months. It became such a pattern, and I became so dependent on it that if I missed being in touch with one of my gentlemen friends one day, it became a source of concern. Two days and I was back on the phone with Veronica panic stricken about what could have happened. I became irrational and paranoid as time went on. This was obvious to Veronica ... I wasn't just a middle aged woman enjoying the company of several male friends ... it had become something other than that.

CHAPTER 11

The user and abuser. Eventually I had to meet one and did. Wayne was the divorced-man-whose-wife-got-the-gold-mine-and-he-got-the-shaft. He was in 'transition' until he could get his feet back on the ground ... living with his parents 'temporarily' until he could do better since his ex-wife kept and lived in their former marital home. What this translated into was that he didn't have a lot of money to spend on dating.

During the brief time I knew him he went from menial job to menial job while professing that, for a long time, he had held an important position at a big airport in a big city nearby. He was let go for a misunderstanding that wasn't his fault. It never is.

I was not so desperate that I offered to pay for dates, but we did spend time together mostly at my place. He seldom offered dinner out, so I usually ended up fixing an elaborate meal and cleaning up afterward while he kept the remote control working. His visits became more frequent with 'stay overs'. He began to bring a few personal things with him and in a short time he actually had more of his stuff at my place than his. His longest 'stay' was three days. By then his computer was at my home and he offered me the use of it when mine was struck by lightning.

One weekend afternoon I turned it on to find 'I' was already signed on. (He had not logged off so I was unknowingly on his account and not on mine.) I checked 'my' email and was shocked to see letters to and from numerous women. By then I realized the computer mixup but having gone this far and taking advantage of his mistake, I read a few of the emails ... one in particular in which he was trying to reconcile with a former girlfriend.

I was sickened by what I saw and instantly did the math. Looking back over our short history, it became crystal clear what was going on. I shut the computer down and started to shake. What to do. I had a few hours before he would be back from work. I wanted him and everything that belonged to him out of there at that very moment.

I had no way of knowing if I was overreacting but I felt assaulted and used. I was also afraid. I had seen an anger streak in him that made me very uncomfortable ... a temper ... road rage a couple of times ... complete disdain for authority.

Wayne had respect for weapons and insisted I buy and learn to use a gun for protection, being alone so much. He helped me pick one out and I could tell by the conversation he had with the salesman that he was very fluent with firearms. An expert marksman himself, he had taken me to the local shooting range several times to learn how to load and use my gun. His ease and familiarity with weapons was always in the back of my mind and subconsciously I vowed to never make him angry ... this would be a real test. By then Edward and I were the best of friends and I knew I could count on his help if I ever found myself in a really bad situation. This counted. I called him and blurted out the whole sordid mess. Knowing how naive I was but never, ever taking advantage of it, he wasn't all that surprised.

Edward thought a few minutes then hatched a plan for me to follow. He told me to print off one of the emails, pack up Wayne's stuff inside the front door and wait. When Wayne came in hand him the email, point to his stuff and then point to the door.

As backup, Edward would come over, park his car, stroll the neighborhood, and a few minutes after Wayne came thru my door, he (Edward) would call me. He would feed me the words to say over the phone so that Wayne would think I was speaking with a policeman. If he needed to, Edward would come in and assist Wayne in leaving.

Wayne was speechless when he came in, but after seeing the email and his stuff packed, he became enraged, turning the table on me ... accusing me of spying, snooping, making me the perpetrator instead of the victim. He did his best to lie his way out and why wouldn't he ... he had had a free ride for more than a few days and didn't want to give it up.

When he realized how determined I was to have him leave and when Edward's well timed call came, he left in a screaming rage, slamming the door with each trip to the car taking a load of his stuff. Edward stayed nearby in the parking lot but didn't have to intervene. When I went to the kitchen window and gave him the prearranged 'all clear' sign, he smiled, waved and drove away. I fell into bed and sobbed ... not for the loss but for myself.

At his invitation, I went to Edward's house for dinner the next night and confessed all. He wondered why I hadn't been available recently; now he knew why. He listened without judgment as I cried my way through the whole embarrassing story. What he did do was talk to me like a trusted advisor and not a jealous or judgmental boyfriend, giving me some very good advice on how to walk through the mine field I was in.

He had been divorced for many years and knew so much about the single scene. He really did care for me and from that moment on, he became the best male friend I ever had. We still dated, but it was different after that because I knew I could really trust him. Also because I was beginning to see so much substance beneath the flashy exterior.

CHAPTER 12

In spite of the burning experience with Wayne, I continued with the juggling act. Edward resumed his calls and never mentioned what happened again. We settled into a very comfortable friendship. I was still 'in love' with him as well.

Married man Eric slowly increased his pursuit, calling and emailing at least once a day. I began to meet him for lunch occasionally. All the talk centered around his unhappiness and I gave him the sympathy and comfort he obviously needed. He came to my condo one day unannounced and it was then that he broke his promise to stay on good behavior.

"Micala, I am so miserable. I am caught in this nightmare marriage and I don't know how to get out of it. My unhappiness is made worse because I now see the possibility of a bright future ... with you. I love you with all my heart ... I need you in my life and I couldn't wait any longer to tell you."

In spite of my promise to myself not to ever become someone's mistress, I finally gave in to his seduction. I couldn't resist him nor temptation any longer. He was elated when I said I loved him too. I was riddled with guilt and self loathing after we consummated our love (or was it just lust or maybe just a mutual need to be needed). He assured me the divorce was in the works and he would soon be free to openly take me places, show me off, show me the world he knew, maybe live together or get married.

After he left, my head was spinning and I was disgusted with myself for sleeping with a married man. Surely I had hit a new low.

My mind told me one thing ... my heart another. I knew this was a no win situation, but I so wanted and needed to believe what Eric said. Early on, I had caught him in a couple of lies. I found out he had taken on a friend's identity (my investigative legal mind was still in top form) and I confronted him about it. He was stunned when I called him by his real name, but admitted his deceit in order to stay under the radar with the pending divorce and couldn't chance my telling anyone about him. He then admitted to having shaved fifteen years off his age and driving different cars all the time. I wondered what other secrets he held from me.

Being naive and more than a little mentally unstable, it didn't make a lot of sense why he didn't trust me with the truth, but he didn't give me the emotional time I needed to put the pieces together. Rather than face the obvious truth, I gave him the benefit of the doubt that lingered in my mind. I was confused about a man who talked of marriage at the same time he was so secretive about the slightest detail of his life.

Wayne actually called and emailed me again, testing my stupid level from time-to-time. Dean called frequently. More and more I let the answering machine take the calls so I could screen who I talked to. I was into this thing deep by then, and what only a few months before had been a thrilling rush had become an emotional roller coaster.

CHAPTER 13

Frequently during calls from Dean, I would experience one of my attacks. How could I explain them to him ... I didn't understand it myself. During 'those' calls we ran thru the same dialogue, time after time.

"Micala, I am really worried about you ... whatever is going on in your mind has been there a long time. I can tell these 'spells' are getting worse. I want to come back ... not back into your life ... or if you want that, then that too, but I want to just be nearby in case you need my help. I am so confused about so much of what has happened and I don't know if I am the cause or the cure for these breakdowns you have."

"Dean ... please don't come back. Whatever is happening, I have to deal with it myself. I can't think straight enough to know what is causing them or to know how to stop them, but with you here I am more confused than ever."

The more I asked him to stay out west, the more convinced he became I was really going crazy (without him?). Was I?

When I didn't hear from Dean for several days, I hoped he had given up on me and decided to stay where he was.

38

One evening Edward came to my home for dinner and as we were starting coffee and dessert, the doorbell rang. Looking thru the peephole, I could see it was Dean. I didn't answer it. He kept ringing it and I had to somehow explain in ten words or less who Dean was and why I wouldn't let him in. Dean started calling me from his cell phone ... over and over, all the while ringing the bell, knocking on my door and shouting to let him in ... he just wanted to check on me.

Caught in this insane scene and not knowing the full background, Edward hardly knew what to do or say. The incessant ringing, knocking, shouting and phone calls didn't stop. Dean could see lights on inside thru slits in the closed blinds so he knew I was there. If I dared to let him in, I didn't know what he might do at the sight of another man ... innocent as it was.

Fritz ran from the door to each window barking, letting me know that Dean was beginning to move around the outside, window to window ... either to see through or open ... I didn't know which. The knocking and calls continued until Fritz ran to the sliding glass door leading to the screened patio. I grabbed Edward and told him we had to hide until Dean gave up and went away.

As we ran to the dark bedroom and sat on the floor, I heard a loud banging sound from the patio and then one that sounded like metal ripping. Fritz was at the bedroom patio door then and when I saw the reflection of a spotlight thru the slats, Edward and I crouched down by the bed.

"Micala, do you have a gun?"

I pointed to the night stand drawer behind us. I whispered that I kept it loaded, and I knew how to use it if I had to. If Dean managed to get inside, I would not hesitate. I knew from the calls, knocking and shouting that Dean was in no state to be dealt with rationally. Whatever his motivation in coming there, he was out of control. Dean continued to shine the spotlight thru the blind slats and bang on the patio door.

As I reached to open the drawer, I heard a slight scuffle on the patio. It was suddenly quiet ... for a long time. The doorbell rang and a policeman announced himself loudly.

Leaving Edward in the dark bedroom, I slowly opened the door to see not only policemen but several neighbors standing around, some crying, some with a look of concern. An alarmed neighbor, and eventually several, had heard and witnessed the commotion and called the police. They had Dean restrained and asked if I wanted to press charges. I hardly knew what to say, but we talked quietly for a few minutes about what had happened.

I tried to downplay it as much as I could, not wanting

to be part of a scene with Dean there in the breeze way but also in court. They had checked the perimeter for damages ... nothing except muddy footprints and the back screen door had been ripped from its hinges. I wanted this to go away as quickly as possible. I told them to release Dean after a strong warning not to come back ever again ... except to clean up the mess he had made and install a new door on the patio the next day while I was at work. If he did that, then this would be over.

Edward stayed in the bedroom during all of this and when I finally closed the front door and walked back to where he was, I collapsed on the floor. He helped me up and we both laid on the bed for what seemed like a long time, just to let the adrenaline drain and recount what had just happened in more detail. This was Edward's second experience with me involving a bad situation with another man. I was humiliated to imagine what he must think of me. I had such a decent honorable life for decades and now it was out of control.

As we lay there in the dark, I began to answer Edward's unasked questions. I automatically tried to put the best spin on the situation and instantly realized what a useless effort this was.

In his normal way of dealing with life, Edward put the

situation into perspective and assured me he had seen things like this happen and much worse. It was part of the 'game' he said ... whatever that meant. In the short span of time between coffee and then, he had pulled enough of the threads together to think that Dean was a jilted lover out for revenge.

After it had been quiet for about a half hour, the phone rang again ... the police were checking to see if Dean had returned. I thanked them for the call and said he had not and to close the books on this matter as I intended to do. Edward left and I collapsed into bed in what I now know was a state of shock.

The next day at work I told Carlo what had happened and he insisted on getting a restraining order against Dean. I immediately dismissed that idea, knowing it would only serve as a challenge to Dean with his disrespect for authority. Then I would have to go through some awful court proceeding to prosecute him for violating it.

When I got home that day, the door had been replaced, the mess cleaned up and I tried to file the event away in my sack of horror stories. My bag was getting full. I didn't know how much longer I could bear the weight of it and still have a normal life ... Hell ... who was I kidding. I was lying to everyone and most of all, myself. I was living anything

BUT a normal life, no matter how much I wished otherwise ... no matter how I tried to 'pretty up' the details.

... THE FULL MELTDOWN ...

CHAPTER 14

Without having resolved some deep rooted emotional defects in my old life, my new life was setting me up for disaster. I was a runaway train looking for a loose rail.

Every day and every night I had come to depend on the calls, emails and dates. I rationalized that it was fun, and it was, as long as it lasted. Whenever it came time to end a relationship ... regardless of which of us did the ending, I went into a state of panic immediately. I should have been sad or remorseful, but it was only stark white terror I felt. I had been having panic attacks ... or episodes as I once called them ... for a very long time.

Whenever emails failed to appear, same thing. Phone not ringing ... same thing. A Friday or Saturday night without plans became unbearable. I began to approach weekends with a terrible dread. If 'they' were not out with me, then 'they' were out with someone else. Same with emails ... same with calls. It was not a feeling of jealousy ... it was far deeper than that. I became paranoid at the thought of being abandoned ... not wanted ... not measuring up to someone else's standard. Failure. It didn't take much to get that train rolling and once it did, Veronica was my only hope ... or

Crossing Bridges and Burning Others ... by Micala Frank.

I began having these attacks at odd times for no particular reason that I could relate to. The demon had a pattern and I knew what it was. I would be in a store or some other public place and sense that all too familiar feeling, or the tears would start, or the shaking. Wherever I was, I finished as fast as I could and got home ... my only haven. I could deal with it in private and I could call Veronica.

Along with being my sister, Veronica is an extremely intelligent, well educated, compassionate person who had been in therapy herself for years. She knew I was in trouble and headed for more. Except for my mother, Veronica had known me longer than anyone else in my life and knew all about me. I would have never felt comfortable talking to my mother about such things ... especially in recent years.

When the first panic attack happened at work, I made an excuse of illness and left. I nearly ran across the street to home and get inside before 'it' started. The second episode at work happened at a time I couldn't leave, so I had to just stay and deal with it. Carlo wanted to know what was happening, and I confided in him as much as I knew. I owed him that much and more ... he had been patient with my moodiness even on the good days ... patient when one of my gentlemen friends would take me to lunch and I came back later than I should have ... patient with what he had come to call my lack of focus. I was making mistakes that I just didn't make ... simple, silly mistakes. I went to work every day with a strong resolve to do better, stay under control and focus on what I was doing. Some days it worked; some it didn't.

The last episode I had at work was on a Friday morning ... I had no plans for the weekend other than housework, errands, and spending time waiting for an email or the phone to ring. The demon reared its ugly head and all I could think of was running away. I had to escape this person I had become. With sincere apologies I tearfully told Carlo I had to leave, that I was going somewhere ... I didn't know where ... but I had to go and I didn't know when I would be back.

Rather than be angry he expressed concern for my bizarre behavior and strongly suggested I not leave town in my condition. Without hesitation, I reverted to the normal mode I had perfected over time ... skillfully learned at the hospital when I was a teenager. Give them what they wanted and they would leave me alone. I only had to keep the act going for a few minutes before he let me go. Why didn't he stop me? I rationalized he didn't care (when in truth he didn't know what to do) and that only made it worse. In my perverted thinking, I was being abandoned again.

CHAPTER 15

Frank ... I would go see Frank. By then we had become very close. I had gone down to see him for a weekend several weeks before, and he had invited me to come back any time I could. We kept in constant contact by phone and emails, and as soon as I got home I called him with the news I was coming down for a visit if he wasn't busy. I became elated when he sounded thrilled that I was coming back.

It was OK then ... I calmed down, stopped the shaking and made hasty preparations to leave. I could make it by dark since I knew the way and if I didn't take too long to get ready. Pack some clothes, call Veronica (deflect her concerns), call the boarding kennel to make reservations for Fritz and Tiger, check my email and phone messages, check locked windows and doors ... everything in order ... load the car (including my gun) and leave. Stop at the drive thru bank to get some cash, get gas, leave Fritz and Tiger at the kennel, another drive thru for a burger and tea, and finally I headed south out of town.

It felt good to sit back and drive familiar road with something nice to look forward to. Frank and I got along so well ... he was calm and pleasant to be around ... just what I needed. The adrenaline began to leave my weary body and as the miles passed, I once again started the futile exercise of trying to understand what had happened that morning and was still happening as I was running away.

I had long since lost control of rational thinking and had moved into a survival mode. I had to do whatever I had to do in order to survive, and this was what I had to do this weekend. Or maybe longer. Or maybe I wouldn't come back for a long time. Or at all. I couldn't think about anything beyond the moment.

CHAPTER 16

Sun was setting when I finally arrived at Frank's home. I was relieved to see him and when he hugged me hello, I couldn't let go. I started sobbing, shaking ... an emotional dam broke inside. He helped me to the couch. He knew this was not going to be a rendevous weekend, but one of rescue. I was the one who had to be rescued and I had put the burden of rescuer on him with no warning.

I had mistakenly thought this weekend would be fun as the other weekends with Frank had been. Instead of leaving my problems behind and escaping them, I brought them with me. I spent most of the weekend curled up on Frank's couch ... at least I was safe there ... but from what I didn't know. I was embarrassed that I had inflicted this on Frank, but at the same time had no controllable choice about it. He stayed with me at a distance, at times talking to me about what was happening.

It was obvious to him I needed more help than he could give and after several days he encouraged me to go home ... if I was able to drive ... and seek medical help. I resisted at first but eventually knew his solution was the only one left. How could I fix 'it' when I didn't even know what 'it' was.

I had given Veronica Frank's phone number and she called several times ... talking mostly to Frank. A couple of times Frank would call me to the phone when they finished. She told me that Dean had been calling her incessantly trying to find me. He was frantic, saying he knew I was sick ... he was the cause of it and he was the only one who could help. Of course she wouldn't divulge my whereabouts.

His calls to her had continued to the point where she asked me to call him, just to let him know I was alive and to stop his day and night calls to her. I drove to a nearby pay phone so he couldn't trace Frank's number and called him. Somehow I was able to force myself into that normal mode I had used in the past long enough to (I thought) convince him that I just needed a change of scene and had taken a vacation to spend with friends. He begged me to tell him where I was but of course I didn't except to say south Florida. He asked me to promise I would call the next day and I said I would if he stopped calling Veronica.

The next day he said he knew where I was and he was coming to get me. I freaked out ... somehow he must have traced the pay phone number. Thank God I had the sense to not call him from Frank's house. This was so unfair to Frank ... to bring this insanity into his life and hope he could fix it. He was so compassionate and caring, but I knew it was far beyond anything he could do.

When I got back to Frank's house and related this most recent call, he had a plan and convinced me to follow it. I had to call the psychiatrist that my doctor had referred me to earlier that spring and make an appointment as soon as possible. I did. He helped me gather my things and suggested he drive me home. I wouldn't let him do that since I had to have my car ... OK, I would drive my car and he would follow and drive back. No, I had to keep this as uncomplicated as I could. I had imposed on Frank's kindness enough ... I would go alone with the promise I would call immediately after I got home.

I took the interstate back, knowing it would be the quickest way. I had to get back to my cocoon and also avoid any confrontation with Dean on the rare chance he showed up at Frank's house. As I drove I sobbed and wailed the entire time. My focus was not what it should have been and when a small trailer towing a car came loose from a motor home in front of me, it was all I could to swerve out of its way. I ended up in the right lane grassy shoulder, far off the road, as did several other cars following me.

I sat and shook for what seemed an eternity, but eventually returned to the highway. Somehow this incident brought me back to reality enough to realize that God had intervened and saved my life for some reason. I drove the rest of the way with a quiet, growing resolve that I had to live ... wanted to live ... but I had a long emotional road back, and where would I start.

CHAPTER 17

When I got home, I found a realtor's card in my door with a note saying she had a prospect who was interested in buying my condo and to please call her. I put it with the rest of the mail that I would tend to later. After retrieving a joyful Fritz and Tiger and unloading the car, I called Veronica and Frank to let them know I was home. I collapsed into bed in a state of exhaustion.

When I woke up (day or night didn't matter by that time) I sat in my recliner a long time reliving what had happened that week and was unsuccessful in trying to make sense of any of it. I forced myself to stop going thru this useless loop and picked up the mail to start sorting it into junk and important. I came to the realtor's card and remembered finding it in my door ... was it earlier that day or last night ... the concept of time was eluding me more and more. I filtered thru some of the mail and then retrieved the realtor's card from the junk pile and looked at it again.

It hit me like a bolt of lightening ... the ultimate solution. The ultimate runaway. I would sell my condo and move somewhere else. The 'somewhere else' didn't matter at the time. It had become a pattern for a quick fix without thinking of the consequences. I rationalized that when you are sinking and someone throws you a life preserver, you don't stop to consider who threw it or what boat they would pull you to for safety. I knew I was sinking fast and this could be just the life preserver I needed.

I would get rid of it all ... all at once ... my home, my job, everything in my past connected to living in this city for over twenty years ... I would start over and leave everything except my stuff and Fritz and Tiger. No. I would store my stuff and just take the kids with me and figure out where I would live later. I had some cash reserve, and this was the time it was meant to be used.

The realtor was very happy to hear from me ... she did have a genuine prospect who had seen a unit with my same floor plan but he wanted something on the ground floor. He was a cash buyer. Perfect. We made the appointment for the showing that same day. I called Veronica and told her about this latest development and how it was the perfect solution. I brushed aside her astonished reaction and practical questions ... no, I didn't know where I would move ... maybe somewhere near Frank ... maybe to Tennessee near her ... all this had happened so fast I hadn't had time to sort out the practical questions, but this was meant to be ... I was sure because of the realtor's card in the door. It was a 'sign'.

She begged me not to pursue this thing with the realtor and told me she was coming down to see me. I told her it really wasn't a good time for a visit for either of us ... it was at the end of her school year and I would be packing and getting ready for a closing. She said she had been thinking about coming down for a visit a long time and she decided this was the time. I told her I didn't want her to come ... my paranoid thinking told me she was coming down to take over and control my life. I knew I had problems, but I would work them out and besides, I had an appointment with my psychiatrist in just a couple of days. I was sure he would agree with me on all counts about relocating.

"Gotta go ... have a lot to do. Thanks for calling and don't worry. This is the solution I have been looking for."

I showed my condo that Saturday afternoon and later got a call from the realtor who said my prospect wanted to make me a full written offer on Monday morning. We set an appointment for 10 ... good, that would give me time to make the 11 o'clock appointment with my psychiatrist ... I might even cancel that appointment since moving would fix whatever was wrong with me.

What I didn't realize was that I would be leaving everything familiar and taking the biggest and only real problem I had with me ... myself.

CHAPTER 18

Veronica called again that evening and I told her what had happened. While we talked the doorbell rang. It was two police officers ... oh my God, what was this all about. They said they were making a 'well being check'. I asked what that was and they said someone was concerned for my safety and asked them to just check on me. Veronica. She had to be the one. I gave them an academy award performance ... forcing myself once again into the normal mode that I knew people found acceptable.

"Yes, I have had some upsetting events in my life lately, but my sister ... if she was the one who made the call ... is so dramatic and overly concerns herself about everything. She lives far away but is coming to visit me soon, so I will look forward to having her here."

I could tell they were buying about half of it.

"No, of course I wouldn't ever think of harming myself ... look at Fritz and Tiger ... I am all they have and I would never leave them. I need them and they need me. Besides, I am a Christian and suicide would mean an eternity in Hell." (Yeah right, like I wasn't living in Hell already.)

They were polite but kept on and on with the questions until I felt like my knees would buckle out from under me. The facade was slipping ... I could keep it together for just so long. Having worked in law for so many years, I knew that at any point they had the authority to take me into custody and have me put under involuntary observation for three days for my own good if they sensed I was a threat to myself or anyone else.

Just when I thought it would all cave in, they gave me their card, bid me goodnight and left. Veronica had heard the entire exchange ... she was still on the other end of the phone.

"How dare you betray me, embarrass me, humiliate me in that way ... it was you, I know it was ... just what other surprises do you have in store for me tonight? Why don't you just call Dean and have him come over tonight as well and we'll make it a real party?"

I slammed the phone down, shaking in anger. I had to get some rest so that tomorrow I could begin to put my mind in order to get thru this move. Before I could get ready for bed, the doorbell rang again. I almost laughed ... what next?

It was Meagan ... a dear friend from my past I had not seen for a long time. Especially lately since I had shut myself off from the world and almost everyone in my past. She said she was thinking about me and knew from our lack of contact that something was wrong. I told her as little as I could politely get by with ... I didn't force myself into the normal mode with Meagan ... she had seen me down before.

Without going into all the details, I told her that Dean and I had parted and I was having a difficult time adjusting to my new life alone (which was true as far as it went). I assured her I had just had a bad couple of days and in time I would be able to get my feet back on the ground. I gave her a sincere hug, told her how much I loved her and thanked her for caring enough to stop by. After she left I collapsed from fatigue and cried myself to sleep. I had been running full throttle with the adrenaline racing for days and weeks. It was about to run dry.

... WIND BENEATH MY WINGS ...

CHAPTER 19

Somewhere in the darkness what little rational thought and fight I had left me. The telephone woke me from something that might pass for a light sleep before it was even daylight. Before I could even say hello, Veronica spoke.

"Don't hang up. Listen to me ... I know you can understand what I am saying. I had to do that last night. I didn't have Celeste's phone number or any of your other friends to call. I called Jonathan but he ..."

"What ... why did you call Jonathan?"

"I wanted someone to visit you ... to keep you company for awhile. Jonathan said he would go but thought his being there would make it worse. Did Meagan come to see you last night?"

"You told Jonathan about my episodes? How did you know Meagan came by last night?"

"My options to help you are getting very limited 800 miles away. Jonathan had kept in touch with Meagan after the divorce and knew that you two were still close friends, so he asked her to go instead. Please don't be mad and please listen. Will you?"

She, Devon and Jade had been up most of the night

talking. Devon was a social worker and Jade was a psychiatric RN, so they had talked about my situation from all angles. The three of them had made a plan and all I had to do was listen.

"I am ready to leave for the train station ... couldn't get a flight ... I will be in Florida late today. Are you able to drive to the train station down town and pick me up or should I take a taxi? Devon, Jade and I all have cell phones with free weekend time. We will take turns calling and talking as long as you want. In fact, you can spend the whole day on the phone with one or the other of us. You can follow my train progress on the Amtrak site."

"Micala, promise me you won't try and figure this thing out anymore. I will take you to your doctor tomorrow and we will start there."

I reminded her I had a contract to sign before the doctor and she agreed that she would take me to that too. She expected a strong rebuttal from me but all I could say was "I will pick you up at the train station. Please hurry so you don't miss the train."

With that, our call was over and so was one of my battles. I had surrendered to whatever demon had crawled inside my mind and finally taken over. It was all I could do to tend to Fritz' and Tiger's needs that day. I didn't open the

60

blinds, shower, dress, eat or make any effort I didn't have to. My home was a mess from the little time I had devoted to it in recent weeks ... dishes, unpacked suitcases from visiting Frank, stacks of mail and unread newspapers. I apologized to the realtor but tried to excuse it by saying I had been away. I didn't tell her that by then I really didn't care how things looked.

All I could do was sit and breathe and knew each passing hour would bring Veronica closer ... she was my only hope. I knew that in the past weeks ... or months ... I had slipped into a living Hell and didn't have a clue how to get back ... or even if I wanted to. I did as promised ... sat and waited and talked on the phone and watched Veronica's train move along on the Amtrak site ... until it was finally time to go get her. I felt a strange sense of relief that someone else would be steering my ship for a while. I was in emotional paralysis.

CHAPTER 20

When I finally heard the train horn blow at the crossing before making the final curve into the station, its lights pierced the darkness and for the first time in a very, very long time, I felt a tiny sense of hope. Veronica was the first one off and I fell into her arms. She led me to the car and drove us both home.

I really couldn't say much after we got home and didn't need to ... what was left to tell her that she didn't already know. She took one look at my condo and it told her everything she didn't already know. I had really lost it. She slept on the couch while I rocked in my recliner, dozing off a couple of times during the remainder of the short night.

The next morning she helped me shower and dress ... made coffee and toast ... took Fritz for a walk and made sure he and Tiger had food and water. She went on autopilot, doing the things that one woman does for another instinctively and without asking ... she put a load of laundry in, put a sink full of dirty dishes in the dishwasher, gathered unopened mail into a stack on my desk, gathered up garbage and unread newspapers to be taken out to the dumpster. She made a delicate attempt to get me to cancel the realtor's appointment, but I insisted, so she drove me. A few papers

Crossing Bridges and Burning Others ... by Micala

signed, and we were on the way to see my psychiatrist.

CHAPTER 21

I remembered very little about the first visit ... Veronica sat in for part of it and gave him most of the information he asked for. I was glad she did ... time and reason had lost its meaning for me and I couldn't have unsnarled my story for him. How could I have told him what was happening when I didn't know myself. Veronica didn't either, but gave him enough that he knew where to start.

Dr. Blair and I talked after Veronica left the room ... he wrote several prescriptions and said I needed to start taking the medication that day. He explained that my treatment would involve a therapy called rapid eye movement and desensitization reprocessing (EMDR for short). He explained how it worked and that I would have a short session that day to test my receptive abilities. I must have passed.

He said that for EMDR to be successful, I had to first help him identify the specific trauma I was experiencing and be able to focus on it as he instructed during the treatments. He asked me to tell him as much as I could and he would ask questions to fill in the blanks. Good. I couldn't make sense of anything. My mind was so fragmented and in such a fog, I was having a hard time identifying my surroundings by then.

I was able to recount the story of my youth and Dean in bits and pieces ... certainly not in the detail I had with Rocky or that I could have done on my own had I not been in this 'well in Hell' as I began to think of my current situation. He filled in the blanks with questions, and that information, along with what Veronica had told him, gave him some basis to work from.

My first session ended with his reminder to take the medicine, and return the next morning at the same time. We would spend that session discussing Jonathan, with whom I had spent over half my life.

"Talk with Veronica this afternoon ... let her help you recall the details of your life with him. If you can, put your thoughts on paper ... or your computer. As much or as little as you are able to. I often advise my patients to write as a form of therapy. It helps them to unlock memories and helps to reconstitute their feelings."

With that he ushered me out to join Veronica, handed her the prescriptions to fill, reiterated the same instructions regarding Jonathan, and told her he would see me again the same time next day. I was exhausted. Veronica took my hand and led me to the car. I felt like a sick child, hoping some grown up could just make it all go away.

A few hours after taking the medication, I was

astounded to see a tiny improvement in my mental clarity. The massive fog was still there, but it wasn't as thick. Veronica and I talked some that afternoon and evening, and I even committed some of what came of it to writing.

Both of us were running on fumes, so she repeated the nightly chores early and we fell asleep right away. I was still in my recliner; she was still on the couch.

CHAPTER 22

When we arrived at Dr. Blair's office the next morning, Veronica asked to sit in for a few minutes. She apologized for forgetting to tell Dr. Blair about this the day before, but it was not a priority. She realized during the night how important it was. She told Dr. Blair about my signing a contract to sell my condominium the day before prior to my appointment with him. She gave him some background information and shared with him that this was just the latest step I had taken in my attempt to run away.

He looked at me with astonishment, an emotion rarely revealed by a psychiatrist. To answer his unasked question when he turned back to Veronica, she told him she had tried to talk me out of doing it. I had insisted and she was afraid to do or say anything more, not knowing what my reaction would be.

"Micala, when you came to see me, you put your faith and trust in me to help you walk thru this mine field. Now I want you to do something to help yourself. I want you to do whatever you have to do to void the contract to sell your home. If necessary, I will intervene with the realtor. You are operating with diminished capacity and are not able to make decisions like that. Your home is the only stable thing in your life right now. That is where you have to start to recover and not run away from."

"Dr. Blair, you are right. I couldn't go thru a move right now if I had to and besides, I have nowhere to go. I suppose it was a desperate act to try and put my past behind me, thinking all my problems would go with it. I will call Carlo ... an attorney and my boss ... perhaps he would be willing and able to fix yet another mess in my life."

He left the room for a few minutes and when he returned, he had a hand written letter for me to give Carlo. He told Veronica and me that we would postpone our counseling until the next morning. He had set daily appointments with me for at least the next week and Veronica would drive me. I had no choice but to do as he said.

CHAPTER 23

"Carlo, this is Micala ... sorry I have to ask for your help when I let you down so unexpectedly. I have done something really stupid. I signed a contract to sell my house and I need your help getting me out of the contract. Yes, I'll be over at four."

Veronica talked to Carlo as she had Dr. Blair and filled him in on the details. I didn't listen. I didn't care who knew what now ... the jig was up, the game was over, the juggling act had come to an end and the circus tent was about to fold up. The clowns had left a long time ago and now all that was left was the mess to clean up ... the ugly, smelly part left behind when all the laughing stops and the people have gone home.

Carlo knew I had been having some really tough times, but didn't know the extent until Veronica filled him in. She also gave him the letter from Dr. Blair. Mostly I just sat and stared at the floor ... partly from embarrassment that the strong capable professional woman Carlo was used to working with had been reduced to this pitiful heap of humanity. Also in part because my medications numbed my pain as well as my senses.

Carlo said all the right things and assured me with a

sense of confidence that he could get my problem with the contract taken care of. He was my knight in shining armor that day. I made no objection when he gently reminded me that in order to fix things, he would have to be candid with the realtor. He made several calls, dictated and faxed a letter to the realtor for her to sign and fax back ... which she did ... and when I left his office I felt a huge sense of relief and gratitude that someone had gone to bat for me and cleaned up one of my many messes that I couldn't.

"Micala, I have to help you get better in my own self interest. You have to keep your home and get well so you can get back to work. I miss you and want you to come back as soon as you can."

Nice compliment ... the thought he wanted me back at work after all the disruption I had caused in his professional life made me feel good. He had confidence I could get better but as he reminded me, it would take a lot of hard work. We were also friends and I knew that my friend, and not my boss, had intervened on my behalf that day. We had been reduced to one human being helping another, the most common denominator on earth.

Veronica took me to a quiet place for supper and we returned home ... my haven which I didn't have to forfeit. She fed Fritz and Tiger and took Fritz for a long walk. The mail, phone messages, chores ... all that could wait as it had for so long. With little talk or ceremony, Veronica helped me get ready for sleeping in my own bed, dosed out the pills, and I fell asleep as soon as I closed my eyes.

CHAPTER 24

Veronica told Dr. Blair the next morning that Carlo had been able to get the contract to sell my home voided. He was obviously relieved and cautioned her to do whatever was needed to keep me from signing anything else until he gave the okay. She waited in the waiting room as Dr. Blair and I began again.

"How do you feel today Micala?"

"I don't know, maybe a little calmer."

"What makes you say that?"

"I am glad Carlo got the contract cancelled. I think some of the medicine is already starting to help clear some of the fog away. I couldn't even think before. I am glad that Veronica is with me. I am glad that you didn't make me go to a hospital to get better."

"The medicine I prescribed is a powerful intervention tool. It acts very quickly. As time goes on, I will adjust your medication schedule, taking away or adding and adjusting dosages to meet your long term needs. For now, just stay with the same routine."

"Do you have feelings of guilt?"

"Oh yes. I feel bad I interrupted Veronica's teaching schedule. I feel bad that I haven't been able to do my regular stuff and she had to come in and clean up after me."

"Can you understand and accept that she wants to make you her top priority now? That she doesn't want or need to be anywhere else right now?"

"Maybe in time I can, but now I am just so sorry ......"

"Micala, if you had cancer and she was here to help with that, I don't think you would feel sorry or guilt. For so many years, people hid mental illness in a closet. It was viewed as a character flaw rather than what it really is ... an illness of the mind, the same as other illnesses of the body. Thank goodness we aren't still in the dark ages where that is concerned, but people suffering from mental illness still feel guilt that they can't cure it themselves.

"If you were taking chemotherapy and she was here to help you, you would willingly accept it. For now, try to think of your treatment as chemotherapy for the mind. You don't need to add an unrealistic feeling of guilt to your list of real mental health issues."

"I'll try."

"Were you able to make some notes about Jonathan, your life with him and the events that shaped your life during those years?"

"When I tried to think about it, I got confused and kept going back over the same things. So I started to write it down

73

and that was easier. In fact, once I really started to write, I couldn't stop. It was like opening a door in my mind. Maybe the medicine helped me think clearer."

"I see you have some papers with you ... is that what you wrote?"

"Yes. I just typed as I thought and found myself typing as fast as I could. My thoughts came so easy and were faster than my fingers."

"Why don't you read what you wrote and I will save my questions until you finish?"

I began reading aloud.

CHAPTER 25

"Jonathan Ashford. The man whose name I took and whose life I began to share less than a year after Dean and I lost contact in the mid 1960's. I can't say that Dean and I broke up; it just became impossible to keep the ship afloat, and shortly before I finished my final, tortuous year of high school, Jonathan rode into my life on his white horse and swept me up into a very placid, quiet place of retreat. I was reluctant at first, but soon surrendered to his charm and tender ways.

"What a welcome feeling it was to step out of my life and into someone else's, if only for the brief times we were together. My days and nights for so long had been spent in fog, a dark fog, a dark, damp fog. It took a long time for daylight to return to my life, but Jonathan provided the key that opened the door just enough for a small sliver of sun to creep in.

"He had a quiet dignity about him that commanded respect. Big in physical stature, his heart was even bigger. I felt like a million little pieces at that time, and Jonathan had a way of helping me slowly pick up each one and re-attach it in such a gentle way, and slowly enough of my Humpty

Dumpty life was put back together again that I could begin to feel something besides pain. It had been a long time since I had shut down inside, and even trusting Jonathan as I did, I could only open the door to my heart just a little. Somewhere in the deep corners of my mind, I knew the only way to keep from getting hit by a truck is to stay out of the traffic. I would not survive another collision, and I did what I had to do to keep it from happening.

"As young as I was, I still knew that people got married for different reasons. I felt so alone, and in spite of Jonathan's cavalcade of friends always around him, somehow I knew that his spirit was as fragile as mine. I knew about one girl who had hurt him badly. I guessed there were more. Maybe he needed me as much as I needed him. Heaven knows I would never be able to inflict the pain on him I had just been through. Until you know what it really feels like to hurt, you can't have any appreciation for someone else's suffering. I had, and I did. I needed to be taken care of, and I needed someone to take care of. Jonathan needed the same things at that time, and so it was within this delicate framework of need that he proposed marriage, and I gladly accepted.

"My storybook wedding took place a few months later,

and for just a brief moment I thought I caught a glimpse of Dean in the shadows just before I started to walk down the church aisle. Surely I was seeing things. I had to put Dean away. In the months leading up to that day I had found a tiny spot in my heart where he could stay, safely, and not intrude into my life. Much as a young girl finally relegates her favorite doll to a corner on the top shelf of her closet, I moved Dean. I knew he would always be there as part of those years, and I prayed so hard for him to have a happy life, whatever that meant. I didn't know how to go about doing it, but I intended to try and find some happiness with and for Jonathan, whatever that meant as well.

"I knew embarrassingly little about life when I married Jonathan. Most of what I had learned about relationships had been warped, and what I had learned had come with a heavy price tag.

"I was totally connected to Jonathan as my protector and at times I found myself standing just to his right and a step behind his elbow peeking out at life. It would take a long, long time before I quit doing that, and it would take even longer before I began to look at Jonathan as my husband and not my savior.

Dr. Blair told me my appointment for the day was

nearly over. "Continue your writing; I would like to take these pages and read them later. Tomorrow we will begin to talk about some of the specific issues involving what you have just read about your early life with Jonathan." With that polite dismissal, I left with Veronica.

I told Veronica about my appointment. She suggested I continue to write; she would take care of Fritz and Tiger, and other necessities, and cook us something for supper. I was beginning to feel emotion again ... relief was the first thing ... that I didn't have any decisions to make. I just followed orders.

CHAPTER 26

The next morning at 8 I was back in Dr. Blair's office with papers in hand. We talked about what I had read aloud the previous day. I answered his questions as honestly as I could. No secrets anymore ... especially not from him ... he was my last hope. As before he asked me to read what I had written.

"Virtually everything I learned about being a grown-up came from Jonathan. At times he acted like a little boy. Often I would catch sight of his profile and saw just a bigger version of a 6 year old kid. He laughed a lot and even when things were serious, he always found something to say to tone down the situation. I loved the way he minimized problems and did what he could to make them go away for me. In all reality I didn't want to deal with anything else bad, sad, ugly or controversial the rest of my life. I never wanted to raise my voice again in anger. I never wanted to shed another tear. I certainly never wanted to ever exchange a cross word with Jonathan. It was not an option. I couldn't imagine anything ever coming between the bond we had begun to form.

"Jonathan was a teacher before we married but was

a builder afterward. He had always been a builder. Back then a builder was someone who knew how to build a house. Simple as that. They knew how from watching and learning from someone else how to do it. Jonathan grew up with a father, grandfather and several uncles who were builders, and he watched and learned from them. As a teenager...and before ... what spare time he wasn't fishing he spent in the woodworking shop his father owned.

"During a few short months I had traveled a road that took me from being a child in a child's world to being a child in an adult's world. This was the big league now and I was like a fish out of water. Jonathan took care of most of the details for the mechanics of life during the first few years of our marriage. Each new day and each new season and each new experience brought with it a little progress for me into the real world. With the passage of time, I began to open up a little more of my soul to let sunlight back in. In doing so and at the same time, I began to step away from Jonathan's shadow. The more I began to rejoin life and take part in things I once enjoyed, the more confidence I gained as a person, something equally foreign came my way to be dealt with.

"With no goal or direction in my academic life, I had

dropped out of college six months after we were married at the time Jonathan received his degree. At last I would now have the time to jump off the treadmill I had been on for so long. With the exciting and scary prospect of my whole life ahead, I would finally be able to settle down to the business of being a new bride, a new wife, a new person with a clean slate and create a new life for us.

"One of the first orders of business to attend to was find and make a home for ourselves in the small hometown we returned to after Jonathan's graduation. At first, I thought the tiny four room house Jonathan located for us to live in was a joke. Windows were broken out, siding falling away, holes in the walls big enough to throw a cat through (I wouldn't do that, but it was the first impression I had of the place), no heat, no bathroom. The house was a wreck. The yard was overgrown with grass, weeds and bushes waist deep. Did people actually live in places like that? I could tell my reaction of stunned disbelief was not what Jonathan was hoping for.

"Being a skilled craftsman, he could see in his mind what I could not -- the potential for something beautiful being created from something so awful.

"I was little help on this project, never having even

held a paint brush, much less saw wood or pound nails. As promised and in only a short time Jonathan turned this place into one of the cutest, most perfect little dream houses in the whole neighborhood. We moved in and began to live like real people before our first anniversary. I loved all the toys that adulthood brought with it -- we had received so many beautiful wedding gifts and at last I had the time, and a place, to bring them all out and enjoy them.

"It was all starting to come together. We were settling into the comfort zone that comes to young married people if they are lucky. A lot of the pain was back there somewhere, getting farther and farther away. Nothing but good from now on. Or so I naively thought.

"Shortly after we had finished remodeling and furnishing our first home and a few weeks into our second year of marriage, our wreck-turned-into-a-dream-home caught fire and was partially burned. What wasn't destroyed by fire was ruined or damaged by water and smoke. Walking around on water-turned-to-ice-floors among the ruins of what only a day before had been so beautiful, I couldn't believe how quickly it had all changed. Both of us felt betrayed -- by what, I don't know, unless fate. It looked so ugly now -- worse even than that first day I saw it. It had become ours.

We had endowed it with part of our soul during the months of its rebirth. I had dared relinquish a little of the fear of life to this place. It had come to represent so much. It housed not only things, but hopes and dreams and trust in the future.

"The ashes were still smoldering when Jonathan began making plans to rebuild. Even better than before, I think he said. The smoke had entered my psyche and created a barrier between what was real and what was not. I knew the fire was real, I knew that a lot of what had been born within that house had died, I felt defeated but so grateful that we had been awakened by the smoke and able to get out of the burning house without any injury to ourselves.

"Somehow life goes on and once again, Jonathan restored the little house in record time. It seemed symbolic that we moved back into it in time to enjoy the rebirth that spring brings with it. The house, the grass, the flowers, and our spirit seemed to come back to life at the same time.

"That same spring of 1965 also brought with it a brief encounter with Dean. During a walk downtown one day, I could see him coming my way. He was different -- in a military uniform -- but his walk and his smile were unmistakable. I was tempted to cross the street before we crossed paths, but it was too late. He had seen me, and it

seemed silly not to stop and say hello.

"Doing fine ... home on leave before going overseas ... heard you were married" .

"He was his usual talkative self, never at a loss for words, but he seemed to have aged far more than the year since our last contact. Words hung in the air for what seemed like an eternity. With the amenities over, what else was there to say but both of us wishing the other happiness in life.

"Odd how old habits die hard. I kept looking around to see if anyone was watching us, but if they were, no one even cared anymore. We were old news by then, to everyone else if not ourselves. We both backed away and once again, I was sure I would never see him again.

Dr. Blair stopped me there. We talked about the fire, and about Dean ... two traumatic events of my young life. The fire got "fixed"; the encounter with Dean only served to open an old wound. As we had done the day before, he ushered me out to meet Veronica after my appointment. I don't know what kind of emotional fuel I was running on at the time, but after meeting with Dr. Blair, I felt both a tiny sense of relief and a profound feeling of exhaustion.

CHAPTER 27

The next morning I went to my standing appointment at 8 and as usual, began reading what I had written the night before.

"At some point in our young marriage, I began to think in terms of our life as a couple rather than two lives being lived by two people. Our life progressed rather predictably over the next several years, punctuated by happy times and sad times. Jonathan and I both worked outside of our home, but this was not enough to take up all the time and energy that we both had. We became involved in things other than our work and gradually became a part of the community we lived in. Nothing spectacular -- no public office or such -- but we did make a contribution in a small way to the betterment of our surroundings through civic, social and church activities.

"Some of the happy times were found in building our first new home. Over time I learned some things about construction from Jonathan and was able to be a contributing part of this project. The biggest lesson I learned was the amount of actual work and the number of hours it took to envision and create a building. This was truly our place from start to finish and the more I learned, the more I wanted to learn. We very proudly moved into and furnished this new home and loved showing it off to friends and anyone else who would come to visit. Humility was not one of our strong suits at that point in our lives. In retrospect, I think we can be forgiven for being as proud of ourselves as we were.

"I wanted and needed to be near Jonathan ... really near him ... for a long time after we married, so I went with him practically everywhere he went except to work. I even did that when Jonathan put together his own construction company. I enjoyed watching things being built and learning how something was made. I watched from a distance and then at night or on the weekends I would try to do what the workers had done. I got a lot of aches and pains and pulled muscles learning how to use different tools and climbing on ladders and mixing mortar by hand, but it was fun. Jonathan never once made fun of me when I tried to do something for the first time. He never made me feel like I shouldn't be doing those things just because I was a woman.

"Another interest we shared over the years was our love of dogs. We took in and adopted as many as we could over time. As with anything of value in a relationship, this was a constant source of happiness mixed with sadness. All of them that we ever adopted were homeless and came with sad stories of their own. The best part was seeing what a wonderful accompaniment they became to our day-to-day lives and what we could do to make their lives better. The worst part was letting go after their lives were finished. Nevertheless, I think both of us wouldn't have changed a thing in this regard. We received far more from our pets than we ever gave them.

"Jonathan and I had decided early on that we would postpone becoming parents until the time felt right for us, and the more years that went by without a family, the more jealously we guarded our privacy. Not a popular concept at the time of our decision, we were always getting hints or asked about having a family. We let people assume what they wanted to and pretty soon, the questions stopped. The decision to not have a family remained one we held onto throughout the years to come until it ceased being a matter we even discussed. Fate often has a way of intervening in decisions like this. It did not in our case, and we did not feel a loss for what we never had.

"Nature, like the government, gives in one hand and takes in the other. We each added new extended family members through marriage and birth, and we each lost others to divorce and death as the years rolled on. We continued to

87

add to and subtract from our treasury of friends as well. Each new change brought with it an adjustment to be made in our minds as well as our hearts. As our souls aged, our scope of involvement widened until we, too, kept up with world events and how they may or may not impact our lives.

"Though it would take many months for the remnants of the Vietnam War to come to an end, many more months before it left our daily conversations, and years for the horror of it all to begin to fade, everyone seemed anxious to turn their attentions elsewhere after it had officially ended in 1973 with the exchange of POWs. Along with being tragic, the war had also exhausted everyone's spirit. It was within this mental framework that people started looking forward to planning for this country's bicentennial celebration. To those born during the 1960's and 1970's, it surely did not mean as much as to those born earlier, of which I was one. It did not escape many people's attention the irony of this event -- the 200th anniversary of this country's freedom -- following so closely on the heels of the experience in Vietnam.

"So many months and years of war had also taken its toll on the brotherhood of Americans. It seemed the bicentennial could be a time to start rebuilding some of the emotional bridges that had been destroyed between us. If there was a general division among two groups of people more so than others, it seemed to fall between the young and the old. The young, in general, seemed to be opposed to the Vietnam involvement. The old, in general, seemed to be in favor of it. Perhaps they were not in favor of the war, but rather in favor of supporting the military's position, whatever it was. I always thought it was oddly reversed from what it should have been: the young men, who had never been to war, should have been more willing to undertake it while the old men, who had seen the horror of it during their generation, should have been opposed to it. Human nature being what it was, I guess the older generation felt they had already made a brave sacrifice and thought the younger one had yet to make theirs.

"Given the perspective of time, I think the younger generation's reluctance to participate was viewed as an act of cowardice. For me, I was terrified of losing a loved one to war, and I could understand the hesitancy of involvement by people of my generation. It was perhaps the first generation in a long time to begin thinking for themselves at an early age, and very simply, they did not want to kill people in a foreign country for a cause they did not understand nor did they want to be killed for the same reason.

89

"In time, though, we all began to put down real and emotional armaments and seemed anxious to have something else to occupy ourselves with -- something happy, something with little or no controversy, something positive, something that would enable us all -- whatever our feelings about the war -- to proudly wave and salute the flag as a nation where before we had been sharply divided.

"I am sure the bicentennial summer of 1976 would have been a much more jubilant experience had it not been for the emotional scars of Vietnam, but it was still an exciting time. Stars and stripes and red, white and blue began to show up everywhere.

"Cities and towns of every size planned activities to mark the occasion, each trying to outdo the other, and church bells rang out across America on the actual day, July 4, 1976. Along with the festivities, the holiday was a solemn and sobering experience for all Americans as historians and the media reminded us of all the sacrifice that those before us had endured to enable us all to have this very proud day. We all knew the experience was temporary, but it seemed, at least for a brief time, we were truly 'one nation under God, with liberty and justice for all'. It was a wonderful time to be an American, flaws and all. The emotional healing that *continues to this day seemed to have been born and taken root during that time.*

I was glad to have Dr. Blair check his watch and with a nod I stopped reading again. It was becoming more difficult each day to pull these memories out and commit them to writing. In the grand scheme of things, the Vietnam War was certainly a more important matter to discuss ... rather, he wanted to focus on 'our' decision not to have children. He knew just how to get to the heart of some of MY most painful issues. Rightly so, since I was there for me. I had to admit that it WAS a decision ... mine mostly ... and not left to chance as I suggested in my writing. Deep inside I was terrified of having children ... not just the physical process, but the commitment it took to raise them.

To be as painfully honest as I could be ... to him and myself ... from my perspective as a child, it didn't seem to me my parents had a lot of pleasure in their lives and rightly or not, I assumed it was because of us kids. The physical, emotional, and financial drain on them must have been tremendous ... or so it appeared to me. I cried real tears that day ... Dr. Blair had hit a terribly raw nerve ... one that was never resolved or healed. Oh it was resolved ... age prevented it from happening by then because of a very early menopause ... but the pain never healed. For years I questioned my decision not to have children ... I was terrified that I would suddenly wake up one day and have terrible regrets about that. I always consoled myself with the thought that I would never miss what I hadn't had.

That day's session ended long after my one hour allotment, but he put ethics before the clock and followed thru with tough issues ... even knowing another patient was probably waiting. I had a small breakthrough that day ... I had allowed myself some emotion ... and once the tears started, there seemed little I could do to stop them. I finally understood Dr. Blair's early admonition to me that 'therapy would be hard work' and I left his office completely drained.

It was Friday and I looked forward to the weekend to just rest. Veronica and I continued to both follow a small routine of necessities, and to go with the flow. We talked very little about what I shared with Dr. Blair ... I couldn't cover the same emotional ground twice in one day. Having spent my emotional energy earlier, mostly it was small talk between us. It had been five days since I started seeing Dr. Blair, and while writing about my life didn't pose a problem, stringing together a coherent sentence aloud had been next to impossible five days earlier.

I could tell the medications were helping. During that first week Dr. Blair had adjusted them up or down, with the intention of creating a good 'cocktail' which would eventually get me to a level playing field ... neither buoyant nor depressed. Each day some of the mental fog lifted, although I was nowhere near to putting the big picture together. Dr. Blair had cautioned me against trying to do this for the time being, so I just focused on one day ... or one hour ... at a time. I had the freedom to do exactly what I felt like doing, whenever I felt like doing it. I continued to write ... at times just a few words ... at times my typing couldn't keep up with my thoughts.

CHAPTER 28

The second Monday I went to Dr. Blair's office was very different from the first Monday. By then we were entrenched in a pattern of finishing any unfinished business from the day before ('clarifying'), my reading, then discussing the 'problem areas' Dr. Blair identified. He assured me that at some point he would have the whole picture put together.

"Sometime during the latter 1970's I bought a poster with a ship on it. Beneath the ship were the words 'a ship is safest in the harbor, but that is not what ships are built for'. It touched something in my soul. I took it home and unrolled it often to read. It seemed to be an invitation to life.

"It was during this time that Jonathan and I found ourselves becoming restless. We had been able to do many things over the years that we had set out to do. We had involved ourselves with various jobs and building projects and hobbies that had brought a lot of hard work, but produced much satisfaction.

"We enjoyed taking part in much our small town had to offer, but something else was growing inside our souls that made us start to expand our horizon. In recent years we had moved from thing to thing with increasing speed, only to

move on once we had reached our immediate goal. We were searching for something.

"The restlessness was coupled with an increasing awareness that there existed beyond our small town a vast world of experiences that we had not been a part of. Jonathan and I had lived within a protective small town cocoon during our years together. There was less risk that we would experience an overwhelming defeat in this place, but also less opportunity for overwhelming success. We didn't want either of these extremes in our life, but we did want the chance to grow.

"During the early part of the 1970s we had started taking annual vacations to Florida for a few weeks during the winter, and each year found ourselves trying to stretch our time away. We found ourselves more reluctant to return home with each trip we made and felt drawn to this world of new experiences. We loved the idea of moving away from ourselves. We loved the lifestyle that we found in a warm climate. We loved the people we met. We loved the thought of starting over -- from what and to what, we were not sure. We were both intrigued by and afraid of the challenge. In spite of life's usual assortment of heartbreak and hardships and pleasures, our field of experience was, and always would be, limited there. We were fast approaching a big crossroads -- perhaps the biggest one yet in our 15 years of marriage.

"We talked about it at length and it soon became the main topic of our conversations. What had started out a stirring of restlessness had become our whole focus by then. We stopped talking about living in Florida in terms of 'if' and started talking about it as 'when'. We soon decided to start the wheels that would some day turn our dream into reality.

"During our next trip to Florida we decided to buy some land on which we would build and relocate after our retirement. This seemed like a pretty safe thing to do; after all, retirement was many years away and surely by then we would have the courage to cut ties and move away to start a new life for ourselves.

"At the end of our vacation that year, we began the three day drive home as proud owners of Florida real estate. It was all we could talk about on the return trip, building dream upon dream, and somewhere along the way, we felt like we were getting farther away from 'home' rather than closer to it. I think we were both startled to realize that emotionally, we had already made the move.

"By the time we arrived back in our small town, we had decided to accelerate our plans by, say, 25 years or so.

We didn't want to wait -- and why should we? We asked ourselves and each other that question over and over, and when neither of us could come up with an answer, we knew our decision had been made. It seemed to make perfect sense: we had spent a number of years working all year to spend a few weeks in a place we dearly loved. Why not reverse the process and spend all year working in a place we dearly loved and take our vacation visiting family and friends back in our home town?

"We kept our plans and dreams to ourselves for awhile. We wanted to be sure before we involved anyone else. We took stock of what had to be done to make such a move and it seemed almost overwhelming. Our roots were indeed deep here -- it was, except for the time away at college after we were married, the only place either of us had ever known. Every part of our day-to-day life involved familiar places and people.

"We hardly passed a car that we didn't recognize or walk down the street without stopping to chat with several people. We knew where to go to get what we needed and had long-standing contacts with our lawyer, doctors, barber, church. We realized we had taken things like that for granted. It wouldn't be the same anywhere else. We would

really have to start over with everything.

As before, Dr. Blair had stopped me and wanted to discuss the move to Florida we were planning. Also as before, he only wanted to know the 'why' of it. I was struggling with an answer and finally told him that it really wasn't one reason, but probably many that all carried equal weight. The weather, certainly ... perhaps to satisfy ourselves that we could really make a life for ourselves far removed from our comfort zone ... to be out from under family expectations ... to become whoever we were meant to be ... the challenge ... the more relaxed lifestyle. Oddly, neither Jonathan nor I had stopped to make a list of reasons ... it was just a conclusion we had both come to at the same time. Perhaps it was none of the reasons I had given Dr. Blair; perhaps it was all and more. Whatever the 'why', I had come to an unwavering conclusion that we were being 'led' ... by God?

I left at the end of my hour and was left with unfinished business and unanswered questions to mull over. Why, indeed?

CHAPTER 29

DAY 7 we began again with one exception. Dr. Blair had extended some of our daily sessions from one hour to two. We needed to cover more ground and he said my writing was an indication that long closed doors in my memory bank had begun to slam open. He wanted that process to accelerate to enable him to identify the demons appearing with more frequency. I wasn't sure I could keep this up indefinitely and not become emotionally dehydrated from the process. Reminding me of his clinical abilities not to let that happen or knowing when to slow the pace or stop it entirely, I nodded in agreement.

"The mechanics of moving from Virginia to Florida were daunting. We had a business, a home, an extra vehicle and probably most of our furnishings to dispose of before going -- and it all had to work at once. We also had to take care of things on the other end -- have a place ready to move into once we arrived.

"We soon realized the mechanics were going to be the easy part. After we made a final decision to go, we started to tell the people in our lives of our plans. We were met with a wide assortment of responses, some positive, some negative. Our families were the most disbelieving -- I don't think they thought we were serious or would ever have the nerve to carry it out. Once we convinced them how determined we were, I think they felt betrayed by our decision. A lot of people took our decision personally, and we had a hard time explaining to them exactly what was driving us to do this. It was somewhat a mystery to us why we felt so compelled to do this, just that it was something we had to do.

"The goal we had set for ourselves, allowing for destiny to intervene, was to be living in Florida by the time we would have taken our next vacation, almost a year away. It seemed like an enormous span of time to wait, given the level of eagerness Jonathan and I had. In all reality, there was more to do than we had realized and in the end, were glad we had set our goal as far ahead as we had. We needed this time to prepare ourselves emotionally and to bring so many relationships to a close. We wanted to continue to maintain family ties and friendships after we had gone, but knew in our hearts that this was not very realistic. It would not be humanly possible on the same scale we had had. After all, part of this process was to close a chapter of our lives as well as open a new one, and we had to let go of some of the past if we were to have the time and energy to build our future.

"It never occurred to us that we would become disenchanted and move back within a few months or year, so we made our plans accordingly, with the intention of going for good. With this determination in mind, we realized that some people we said our final good-byes to would be just that -- the last time we would ever see them. We didn't know who would be among that group, but knew some would. As sobering an experience as this was, we began to see it as an opportunity that few people had in life -- to know that the last time we saw someone before our move could very well be the last time we ever saw them again. We took advantage of these experiences to relate with and relay to all these people what each one had meant to our lives. Because of this level of honesty and candor, the weeks before our final departure proved to be some of the richest and yet most bittersweet experiences either of us ever had.

"We were not able to accomplish everything we needed to do within the year allotted, so decided instead to move to Florida for a trial run of about three months at the time we had originally set for our permanent move. We took what we thought we would need to live, closed up our home, and departed. It also allowed us to have a trial separation with our previous life. If living in Florida as residents and not as tourists was not what we had expected it to be, we could always come back and with some adjustments, return to our old life. It was with this reassuring thought that we set out on a journey that would change the course of our lives forever.

"All this time I had seen the little boat docked in the harbor, and suddenly I began to see it moving away from its moorings, very slowly and with some apprehension, but moving, nevertheless. Where would our little boat dock next? What kind of voyage would we have? Was the boat sturdy enough to make the journey or would it capsize as some of our friends predicted? What lay just beyond the horizon that we could not now see but only imagine?

"Jonathan and I were still mystified by the determination and excitement we felt about our new experience. Of course we were filled with mixed emotions about leaving behind so much of our life, certainly everything that had been comfortable and familiar. There were brief moments when the reality of what we were doing would settle into a corner of our minds and cast a shadow of doubt over our lives. Neither of us understood what had almost become an obsession to make this journey, only that we had to do it. The sheer challenge of it was more than either of us had ever experienced and it was exhilarating.

"As expected, once we arrived in Florida we encountered a lot of adjustments. We had anticipated some of the more obvious ones, but had no way of anticipating many others. We had tried to prepare ourselves for what we knew we would find, and also for what we didn't know.

"We didn't expect to find a big welcome banner upon our arrival, but neither did we expect to find some of the open and blatant hostility we encountered. Small towns have a reputation for being hard on newcomers -- the big town we settled in had it all over a small town in that department. Eventually we did meet and become good friends with some of the finest people we ever knew.

"In time, we understood why newcomers were viewed with some distaste. We were encroaching on the native's territory. The newcomers as a group -- literally thousands every year -- were putting a strain on the state's resources and crowding into areas that were probably never meant to be lived in, at least by people.

"We were polluting, using, wasting, populating, expanding, creating urban sprawl, and encroaching on not only their territory but nature's as well. Folks already living in Florida couldn't see a lot of benefit to be gained from all the newcomers, but felt most of what they brought with them was attitude and accents and bad manners. Some of that feeling was justified; some wasn't. After all, the land didn't belong to anyone regardless of what their deeds said, and at some point in history, everyone had been a transplant from somewhere else.

"After a couple of false starts toward adjustment, we did settle into somewhat of a day-to-day routine of living like regular people -- whatever that meant in Florida we had to find out, and that was why we were here.

"We were staying in very humble surroundings for the time being: an extremely small older house we had purchased as an 'interim' home. The house had just been renovated and actually was quite comfortable. We had a minimum of furnishings, but enough to take care of basic needs. Jonathan took a temporary job and I spent my time taking care of our surroundings and getting to know our neighborhood and new city, and eventually even take some classes at the local community college. We intended to use these months as a time of discovery and trying to learn just what it was that was drawing us here so fiercely.

"Indeed, it was very different from what we were used to. Not much about our day-to-day life was the same. It did feel strange to not be recognized by people we met on the street, in stores, in restaurants -- anywhere we went, we were strangers and treated as such. A simple task like getting a haircut or paying for groceries by check was a whole new process. The weather was certainly different. We were at sea level now. Our hometown was at an elevation of 4100'. Living within a mile of the seacoast now, we had constant breezes and very high humidity, both of which were noticeably different for us. The most significant adjustment to weather was the temperature. Except for when we were there on vacation, temperatures in the '70s and '80s during January and February were not what we were used to.

"In spite of the meager surroundings and adaptations we had to make, Jonathan and I found ourselves strangely content for the first time in a very long time. We were convinced that destiny had some purpose in our being where we were and that in time we would understand what it was. We relied on each other more than before.

"We didn't have endless meetings to attend nor did we have family and friends to spend time with or distract ourselves. For the first time ever, we had free time that wasn't earmarked for work or some other project. We began to relax and enjoy some of the benefits of Florida living, like trips to the beach or fishing jetty or just being out in the yard talking with neighbors in the evenings.

"Long before our three month trial stay drew to a close, we knew that, in spite of the different world we had found ourselves in, Florida was the place we needed and wanted to be. We found a certain camaraderie among other transplants. It was fascinating that, regardless of the varied backgrounds from which everyone came, everyone came with something of a clean slate. People moved to Florida for one of two reasons: either to get away from something or to go to something, and sometimes a mixture of the two. Once here, everyone had to start over in one way or another. For some, the task proved to be too much and they went back disenchanted or disillusioned or just plain homesick. For others, it proved to be just the catalyst they needed to either get on with life or begin rebuilding a new life.

"We anxiously returned to our hometown to finalize plans for our final move. Our only remaining major task was to sell our home. All the other things had been accomplished before our trial move a few months earlier. We did sell our house quickly, and at that point, we did experience some real trepidation. Luckily, it didn't hit both Jonathan and me at the same time, so we could each reassure the other when the doubts did come. All that was left were minor details.

"The remaining few weeks we spent in making final visits with friends and family to say our good-byes, closing out bank accounts, readying our vehicles for the trip.. We still couldn't answer with any clarity why we felt so compelled to make this move, or what we were going to do once we got there. No one in either of our immediate families had ever undertaken such a venture before without definite plans. Each person had their own idea of why we were going, and I suppose, each person was right in a way. In truth, there were many reasons we wanted to make this move, but also knew that destiny or fate or divine intervention played the pivotal role in all this. Had it not been for that, neither Jonathan nor I would have had the courage or desire to make this kind of change in our lives. Most of the people in our life had led very traditional, conservative lives; we had ourselves. I think at that point, we were viewed as mavericks at best and reckless at worst.

"On the day before moving, I walked through the skeleton of what had, for seven or eight years, been our home. I was almost overcome with emotion. It was too late now to turn back, and I really didn't want to, but it was at last time to actually begin turning plans into reality. The yard and gardens were so beautiful. This had always been a love of mine -- *growing things, especially flowers, and Jonathan and I had literally put our souls into this place -- inside and out. We had thousands of plants and bulbs and shrubs that we tended to and enjoyed each spring and summer, and now, in early autumn, I would be leaving it all at the height of its beauty. I foolishly wondered if they were putting on their most glorious show as a farewell gift.*

"I needed this private time, before the movers came the next day, before friends and families came by to say goodbye, before it was time to hurriedly clean the floors and lock the door, before it was time to round up the dogs in the vehicles and drive away. I needed this time to go from room to room and flowerbed to flowerbed and remember all the work I had put into and the pleasure I had received from, all these things. I needed this private time to say goodbye to everything that had been so familiar in my life for all of my life. I remembered the hard work Jonathan and I put into building this place, the hardships and the joys we had encountered in creating our home. Memories that I had almost forgotten came flooding back from some corner of my mind to sting my heart and soothe my soul.

"As we lay on a borrowed air mattress trying to find sleep that night, Jonathan and I each dealt with our own

thoughts. *All the words had been said. All the plans had been made. All the things had at last been done. I revisited that small corner of my mind that wondered why we were doing this. We weren't going because of a job transfer. We weren't going to escape a hideous past. We weren't going to be near family. We were leaving all we knew to go 1,000 miles away where we knew little, by free will. Or was it?*

"*Before I left, I gave my poster to Veronica. I think it meant as much to her as it had to me. My boat was so small and the sea was so big, but I knew I had moved well away from the harbor and could not turn back now. I couldn't understand the words, but I did hear it speak. Its call was irresistible and it beckoned me to go with it. I did.*

I stopped and looked at Dr. Blair. He had stopped taking notes as I read and sat with arms crossed, staring at me. Neither of us spoke for what seemed minutes (although his time was too valuable to waste like that). He was intrigued by our move from everything we had ever known to total anonymity.

"Jonathan wanted to move down here at much as you?" I assured him we were equally nearly obsessed with the idea.

"Do you know if you were running from something or running to something?"

"Probably some of both." With that, the day's session ended.

CHAPTER 30

DAY 8, the regurgitation of my life continued.

"We, along with our hopes and dreams, arrived in Florida the autumn of 1980 anxious to start this new life. Our anticipation was matched equally by apprehension. Had we completely lost our minds? What in the world were we doing here? We had disposed of so much of the material part of our lives and what we had remaining became a small caravan of two vehicles with two people, dogs, plants, and a moving van of some furniture, memories, mementoes, everything we owned. It occurred to me sometime during this trip that a wreck could wipe it all out and there would be no evidence of us or the last fifteen years of our lives.

"Once we arrived, we had little time and energy to devote to any feelings of doubt and misgiving. We jumped head first into establishing a place for ourselves in that big city. We hadn't been there long until that old feeling I had when I entered college of going from being 'a big fish in a little pond to being a little fish in a big pond' returned. We had been warned by some of our friends who had moved away years ago from our hometown to big city life that we should be prepared for some real adjustments. They were

right.

"Right away, we had to learn where not to go; the areas not to drive into; rules of the street about where not to walk after dark and where not to walk day or night. Where it was okay to drive in certain areas during the day, but don't stop at corners or red lights if they could be avoided; where it was okay to shop ... not okay to shop ... what part of the beach was safe during the day ... which part of the beach was not safe at any time... it started to sound more like a military encampment rather than our new hometown. There seemed to be more 'don'ts' than 'do's'. We had learned some of this during our trial run back in the spring, but this was the real thing.

"Making as many allowances as we could for this being a completely different lifestyle than we were used to, we nevertheless began having reservations early on about the place. We deluded ourselves into thinking it would be that way anywhere we went. There were probably rules just like that for the small town we came from ... we just grew up with them and did, and didn't, go and do things there without thought.

"Determined not to let fear rule our lives, we went ahead with plans to build our new home and get on with life, with whatever limitations there were to living in the big city. Luckily, the few contacts we had made through reference and 'friend of a friend' were good ones and we were not taken advantage of, or overly so, by the people who helped put our dream home into place. At the same time Jonathan starting working with a very good statewide company in construction related sales. Odd how he always thought he wouldn't be good at sales. Once he got into it and learned the area, he was a natural and eventually would become recognized statewide as one of their top salespeople.

"It seemed all our highs were matched by lows in our new environment. We were nearly ready to move into our new home and really start planting roots when we encountered what would eventually become our undoing there. Lots were small so houses were close. So were yards, and to make matters worse the lots were 'back-to-back' on this street -- as they were on almost all the streets in the city. Many of the people in our near proximity had little else to do with their time than pick flaws, find fault, pick on the newcomer on the block and whine about 'the way things were done up north'. Why in Heaven's name didn't they just go back up north where they came from -- I eventually reminded some of them that the road that brought them into

113

Florida could just as easily take them back.

"I was not used to having to defend everything I did or had. Some of the neighbors hated dogs. That was one area that you didn't get into with this small town girl. I found myself becoming the person they were. I had never had such unpleasant experiences in or with a neighborhood in my entire life -- didn't matter where everyone was from, 'they' were better than anyone else and 'they' had more of a right to be there than anyone else. I couldn't believe these people were living here in this kind of environment day-to-day. Some of them actually thrived on it. Some of them needed to get a life. It didn't take long before it reminded me of rats in a cage -- an overpopulated cage -- each rat staking our territory and snapping at every other rat that even came near.

"Things did not get any better after we moved in; in fact, they got worse. In the midst of the collective temper tantrums everyone seemed to be throwing all the time, my one and only bright spot came in the form of the neighbor across the street whom we had met while building. Madeline -- 'Mattie' – became a wonderful friend to me, and she got into the habit of coming over every afternoon for a few minutes just to see what the zoo was up to that day. Where I let it get to me, she found real humor in all the antics. A

very outspoken and opinionated person who could, when need be, yell with the best of them (she even had all the right hand signals).

"She took me under her wing for some reason and tried as best she could to give me a crash course in survival. When I tried to understand what was happening and make sense of it, her response was to just get in there and give as good as I got. I wasn't a saint, but I just had no experience in that kind of debate and didn't think I could learn fast enough to swim with these sharks. I knew I would sink if I even tried. Mattie was a generation older than I and her age and background gave her a veneer that was as hard as nails and earned through many of life's most difficult experiences through the years.

"I really wanted to be a part of this new world around me, but something told me Jonathan and I were going to be like square pegs in round holes no matter how long we were here. People grouped together. There were clubs here for people from different states, the 'Ohio Club', the 'Virginia Club'. Silly me, I thought people moved down here to be a part of the 'Florida Club', and not to just drag that part of their life along with them. Not only states, but religions and ethnic backgrounds were cause for division, and each group disliked or hated another group or groups. I was having a hard time keeping it all straight and as ridiculous and tragic as it seems to me now, at that time I took it all very seriously. Jonathan and I must have looked like the small town bumpkins that we were.

"After a few months of non-adjustment, I thought that getting out and going to work might be the thing that would help get me away from the day-to-day tedium. I did but it didn't.

"The lighter moments of neighborhood antics were not to be believed. Mattie found these characters cause for great hilarity. I was more bewildered by them. Our street alone provided many true stories -- who knew how many there were in the entire city. Had I not seen some of the craziness with my own eyes, I wouldn't have believed it myself. The fellow who lived behind us (cross my heart and hope to never live on his street again) hosed his roof down -- repeatedly -- while it was raining -- with a garden hose -- while standing on the roof.

"Or the fellow who, every night as regular as clockwork, stood in his backyard and practiced 'whooping'. I never knew why and was afraid to ask anyone else in this collective fruit bowl about it.

"This must have been where the term 'giving someone their space' originated. Not only ground space, but air space as well. One of the neighbors had a fruit tree that hung over a neighbor's fence and occasionally dropped a fruit into the neighbor's yard ... not watermelons, but two inch fruit. Instead of being grateful for food literally dropping out of the sky, the receiving neighbor was constantly yelling at the offending fruit tree owner neighbor to keep his fruit and his tree to himself. I thought he was joking until I saw fruit flying through the air back into the tree owner's direction.

"That did it, right then and there, enough was enough. Never mind certain parts of town being off limits during the day -- or was it during the night -- or was it safe to drive through but not walk through -- hurling fruit grenades took the cake. I simply would not put up with it any longer and my ability to find any humor in any of it was gone -- drained -- tapped out.

"Adios amigos.

"Jonathan and I had to admit that while the dream had not been shattered, it had been cracked significantly. We were not going to give it up, just make changes to it.

"With much sadness, we decided that we had docked our boat at the wrong port. As tourists, we had seen an entirely different side of the place we were trying to call home. Making a living and interacting within a community on a day-to-day basis was not the same as coming as a visitor and seeing the inside of motel rooms and restaurants. We lived in an entirely different part of town than where the tourists gathered.

"The worst part was trying to deal with the sleazy side of life that was new to us. Never mind the wacky neighbors; I am talking big time crime here. There indeed was crime where we came from but not on the grand scale it was here, nor was it almost all drug related. Being a coastal city, it was all around us. Even at the beach; most especially at the beach. This was a very serious and dangerous side of life we had no experience with whatsoever, and it was a side I would just as soon not have to live with.

"We decided to heed our own advice about not complaining and simply let the road that brought us here take us back -- but only part of the way. Florida was still the place we wanted to be. All in all it was a beautiful place, with beautiful weather, and always so many things to do. We just needed to live in a smaller town, one that was not so cosmopolitan, so diverse in its culture, one that we would be better suited to. So it was with a list of transfer possibilities for Jonathan that we set out, once again, to find a place to call home.

"After several weekend visit to the places available to us, we decided to begin again in a smaller town in the north central part of the state. It is hard to say exactly what draws you to a place, and I couldn't really say what brought us to the place we finally settled in. It just felt right. At the same time, it was so ironic because we had not been impressed with the place as tourists -- mainly because it was a small place, was inland, and didn't seem to have the glitz, the sparkle. the razzle-dazzle we had come to associate with Florida. We came to realize that much of the razzle-dazzle of big city life often translated into 'doing time for doing crime'. We had no interest in integrating into a society that had so much of that element to it. Big city life brought big city problems. The advantages were not worth the price.

"Without a doubt the hardest part of saying goodbye was leaving our new house. We had dreamed about it for a long time, and lived in it only a few months. There was nothing to do but put it on the market and hope for a quick sale. Luckily, this very thing happened and within just a few short weeks, we had finalized all the details necessary to make the move 'north'. One year to the day that we made the permanent move to Florida the previous autumn, we moved once again.

"Within the previous 21 months, we had moved 5 times, and 2 of those times had been to Florida from our home town up north, some 1,000 miles away. We felt like the 21 months since deciding to move to Florida had been spent on a teeter-totter. Up and down, up and down.

"Jonathan and I had allowed ourselves the luxury of buying a new, finished spec house in our new location, one that we could just move into without building or remodeling in some way ourselves. In fact, except for the small apartment we had a few months after we were married, this was the first place we had ever lived that was completely finished when we moved in. We almost felt like we were cheating, but it was just what we needed at the time.

"We were weary from our experiences the previous year or so. There indeed were many problems in the big city, but we had to admit that some of them were with us. I suppose there were more problems with our ability to deal with them. We had tried to make too big a step all at once, coming from such a small town.

"Before the moving van was unloaded, some of our 'new' neighbors had come calling -- not only to welcome us to the neighborhood, but to bring us our first meal ... some of the birthday barbecue they were cooking outside. They offered help, friendship, tools; anything we needed to get settled in, they were willing to help. After they left, Jonathan and I stood there with all our hands full of plates of warm food, and just stared at each other for a long time. The reception we had received here compared to the one we had received a year ago was stunning in contrast.

"I think that single experience set the pace for our new life in our new town. Everywhere we went we encountered the same warm, friendly attitude among people. Things were certainly different here. Had Jonathan and I not had the year's detour elsewhere, we would not have had near the appreciation for what we found here. For every unhappy experience before, it seemed we had a good one here. It was amazing. We couldn't get over the difference, and we were so grateful for whatever guiding force it was that brought us to this place.

CHAPTER 31

DAY 9 began with the same routine. I was glad the weekend was in sight; I was growing weary and exhausted from the writing and all the memories it brought back. As always, Dr. Blair busied himself taking notes as I read aloud, stopping me along the way to clarify something.

"The next few years were calm and full of routine, which we had come to appreciate enormously after all the moving, packing, unpacking, building, and turmoil we had in recent times. Jonathan was very happy with his work and more successful than ever. An outgoing person by nature, he made friends everywhere he went and in retrospect, this was one of the best times of his life.

"In years past in whatever work he was doing, I had worked alongside Jonathan, in addition to being employed myself. We had worked as a team in the construction or construction related work he had always done. There was really nothing I could do for him in this line of work, so for probably the first time in my life, I was left to decide my own fate and future.

"Real estate sales seemed a natural step for me to take. I went back to school, completed the necessary course

and passed my state board exam on the first try. I was thrilled with my new accomplishment and at 34, it gave me the self confidence I needed to embark on my first independent venture in my life. New town, new house, new friends, new career. It seemed like a fresh start all around. It didn't happen -- at least part of it didn't.

"Just as well suited to a sales career as Jonathan was, I was not. I had gone to work in a very reputable brokerage, but soon realized I did not have the qualities necessary to make any kind of a career of it. Shortly into this realization, I changed directions again and used my experience and recent education to begin working for a real estate attorney. Just as the move to our first Florida location had been a false start, so had my very short career in real estate sales been. I had no regrets; things had worked out for the best after all.

"This time in our life brought us the first real loss either of us had had in our lives. Jonathan's mother had been in failing health back in Virginia and shortly before Christmas that year, she died. We had been back to see her only a few days before. We both knew it was our last visit, though we had no idea it would be just a matter of a few days until her death. Time and perspective later persuaded us to believe she waited until we came for that visit before letting go of life. She had been a very determined person in other aspects of her life; why not this last one.

"I learned so much about life from her; more than I realized until years later when I would come to hold her in the highest regard. I haven't canonized her in my mind or my heart, but have wished more than once I had had more years with her than I did. I learned that all the good qualities that Jonathan had, he got from her.

"The only other thing to bring real sadness to this otherwise happy time was the loss of our first pet: a big, shaggy mutt with liquid brown eyes who had won our hearts as a sick, sad stray some 13 years before. The vet had said he was about 2 when we found him, so that made him 15 when he died. Even knowing he had all those extra years didn't ease our sadness when he finally crossed over the rainbow and took his place in our memories.

"Having never experienced the death of a pet before as an adult, I didn't know how to get over that kind of loss. He had indeed been a very special part of my life, as all my pets over the years had been. It left a small permanent hole in our hearts. We did what we could in giving him a final resting place, made a monument, framed some pictures of him, and asked ourselves the same question everyone who has ever loved a pet asks -- will he be there waiting to greet us if we are good enough to get to Heaven?

"A few years after our relocation, restlessness crept back into our life. It had happened so many other times to us, and I didn't understand why that just when things calmed down and smoothed out, I or we were overcome with this urge to make changes. I think we needed new challenges.

"Jonathan and I decided to build again and set out to find just the right spot to build yet another dream home. This one would not be like the first one we built down here. That one was very small and better suited to a more tropical lifestyle. We convinced ourselves we needed to expand our surroundings to be more in keeping with Jonathan's phenomenal success in his career. We had unknowingly come to this city when it was on the edge of an explosive population increase. In the intervening years, it would double in population, and Jonathan was at the right place at the right time when it all began.

"Whole subdivisions were platted and opened up within weeks of each other. Model homes were being advertised everywhere to entice the wave of newcomers. New roads were being cut through huge horse farms which were subsequently subdivided into entire new communities. What had been country roads within just a few short years became four and six lane major thoroughfares with all the attendant growth springing up along the roadsides.

"Restaurants, shopping centers, motels, huge construction discount warehouses opened up, every imaginable chain store wanted a location here. Traffic jams were a sign of the times. Four lane roads could no longer hold the traffic that only a couple of years before had been two lanes. Everyone talked about growth, expansion, prosperity, boom times. In just a few years time, our small town grew to be bigger than the big city we started out living in. We stayed and thrived. One factor that made the difference here was that to a great extent, the crime rate did not parallel the population growth. Jonathan and I also grew with the town.

"More people meant more houses. More houses meant more supplies to build them, and Jonathan's career was in selling these supplies. The wave of good fortune built to a point that it even frightened Jonathan. He was working very hard, but he had never dreamed of such success. What he did not know was that the seeds of destruction were being planted in this garden of dreams. It would take a few more years before they germinated and grew into full bloom, but he and we planned our future lives based on our current good fortune.

"Jonathan knew every person in the construction trades here so he was able to pick the best of the best to build our new home. It was much more than we would ever need -- 3 bedrooms, 3 baths, a full game room, library, walk-in pantry, eat-in kitchen, a living room we could hold a square dance in, dining room, an office, porches, garages, a full workshop building for Jonathan, landscaped courtyards, fish ponds, fountains, all set on several acres with a natural spring-fed bass pond in the front yard almost an acre big itself.

"Though neither Jonathan nor I had come from a luxurious background and neither of us had grand aspirations, this surely was more than we had ever hoped to have. It was a symbol to us of not how much we had, but as a reminder that the hard work we had done all those years had indeed paid off.

"We had a few years of tranquility in our new home, but nothing lasts and this didn't either. Reality pricked at our bubble once again and brought us back to earth. Plans were revealed that the wonderful company Jonathan had worked

127

for all our years in Florida was being taken over by a foreign concern. We had heard takeover rumors several times in the past, but none of them were true. Until this one.

"No one knew just how this would affect employment practices, but few people felt the changes would be for the better. It had been a great place to work then and change could only be for the worse. It didn't take long for Jonathan and many others to become disenchanted with the reorganization process. He left the company, went to work elsewhere, went back to the company, then left a second and final time. He, and so many others, wanted things to be the way they used to be, but it didn't happen. Those days were over. About the same time, the remarkable building boom started to overtake the population growth and there was a slowdown in construction. Taken together, these two factors, coupled with Jonathan's new job requiring long distance traveling, made us take a hard look at our life. Once again, we needed to make adjustments to accommodate the circumstances.

"The first thing we needed to do was to scale down our lifestyle significantly and move back into a less rural area for my safety during Jonathan's absences. We sold our dream and the home went along with it. There really was no bitterness, just a feeling of sadness once again at leaving part of ourselves behind, and disappointment that we were, once again, in the hands of fate. We were both in our '40s by then and we had spent every free minute taking care of the house and grounds by ourselves. In all reality, what in the beginning had been our pride and joy had become a burden to take care of. Besides consuming all our time, it had become a financial drain to keep up.

"Uncertain as to what direction our life would take next, Jonathan and I bought ourselves some time by buying a small, older home where we could live until we made up our mind. It was structurally sound and livable, but needed a complete cosmetic updating. We began remodeling a room at a time and enjoyed being in the midst of yet another big project. One thing led to another and we spent the next year and a half painting, wallpapering, installing carpet, wood and tile floors and bringing the twenty year old landscaping under control. It ended up being a very nice little home, and it was easy to maintain once finished since we had taken two of the three bedrooms for nothing but storage. We had brought virtually everything with us from the big house since we were reluctant to scale down our furnishings until we knew what we would need in our next home.

"Jonathan continued working out-of-town in his traveling job and when he was home, we spent a good deal of time discussing our future. We were beginning to tire from all the years of hard work and Jonathan was becoming weary from all his time on the road. We had a big decision to make, which we kept postponing -- whether to reinvest in another big house or stay where we were and pay capital gain taxes. We didn't have to do anything if we decided to stay there, but if we decided to reinvest and move again, we had to have it completed no later than two years after we had moved in. Time was the critical factor in our deciding.

"The passage of time forced a decision. I don't know what the deciding factor was, but at last we decided to build again. Having been through this together so many times before, I was able to step in for Jonathan quite a bit, especially in the paperwork and coordination phases of it. We drew plans, we lined up a building contractor to oversee the work, and we had made our financing arrangements when work began six months before our deadline.

"For good and for bad, we got a sale for our interim house shortly after we started building. Good because we wouldn't have to carry two mortgages; bad because we didn't have the new house to the point we could live in it. We put everything into high gear and barely got our certificate of occupancy the morning the moving van was to arrive. Besides easing the financial burden, at least we wouldn't have the burden of taking care of one place in addition to building the second one.

"The down side to all of it was that we would be living in a house that on the outside looked finished, but on the inside was barely habitable. We lived on concrete floors with only a small bathroom completed. The kitchen had cabinets but no counters or stove. Throughout the house, most of the light fixtures and other outlets had been capped off until we had time to install them. None of the interior doors were installed nor did we have trim on them or the windows. We lived in two of the rooms while we finished the others. Once we got in we felt our first real ray of hope that we would make our deadline. At least one of the two requirements had been met: we were living there, and we might just finish it in time if we could devote virtually every free minute of our time for the next three months to this project. We couldn't. Fate had other matters for us to deal with.

CHAPTER 32

DAY 10 ... Friday. I had been following this same routine day in and day out for two weeks. Dr. Blair had set my appointment for mid afternoon today. He wanted to finish gathering my history and spend the weekend reviewing it. Monday, he said, he would have a plan. First would be the diagnosis and next, a fixed medication regime he wanted me to stay on, and third, we would begin the actual therapy. I was glad to come to the end of this process. I had shed many tears during my writing and reading, and at times felt like I couldn't go on with either. The memories were, for the most part, sad ... not just sad memories, but the recall was very painful and sad. I wanted this part of my life laid to rest ... perhaps I was in some way giving it a proper eulogy by retelling it aloud from my writing. At this point I could do nothing to change any of it and all I could see myself doing was taking one step after another backward.

"Jonathan's father died rather suddenly the week after we moved in. The stress level that Jonathan and I both had been under for the past three months had been very high, and when the call came, it just about caved us both in. We did what we could just to secure the house, make only the minimum of preparations for being away from it and our jobs,

and the next day begin that long journey north to our hometown in Virginia. The two day car trip provided an enforced rest for Jonathan and I. We used those quiet hours to try to prepare ourselves for what we had to face, emotionally, once we reached our destination.

"As we knew it would be, Joe's funeral was a wrenching experience. Everyone knew Joe exemplified the phrase of 'marching to his own drum', and that included the way he isolated himself from friends and family after Jonathan's mother, Grace, died. By his choice, he and Jonathan had grown apart after her death. Joe came from the old generation of being a 'man's man' which included never being emotional or emotionally dependent on anyone. Any attempt we made to communicate with Joe was quickly and stingingly rebuffed by him. As much as it hurt my feelings, my heart ached for Jonathan, who had made numerous attempts to reach out to him, never missing a birthday or holiday remembrance, and keeping in touch with calls and visits. Joe never did return the favor to either of us.

"In all reality, I think Grace's death nearly killed Joe as well, although he certainly couldn't admit it even to himself. Never a spiritual man himself, he never passed up an opportunity to ridicule a person's religion to their face. He didn't put any stock in theology. He had relied on his own doing since he left home as nothing more than a child himself. In his way of looking at things, he viewed faith in God or anything spiritual as a sign of weakness rather than strength.

"He also had no use for anyone who didn't think exactly the way he did about things, which ended up being just about everyone. It might have been better for Joe if he had joined Grace sooner, because the eight years he outlived her were miserable, bitter, hateful and angry for him -- and for anyone who came around him. Not once in those years did Jonathan get a gift, a letter, a Christmas or birthday card, or a telephone call from Joe. An end of an era was buried with Joe that early June day and I think everyone who was there to bid him farewell felt he was finally where he had wanted to be for some time.

"After spending as many days as we dared to, we returned home exhausted, facing even more stress than we left. Jonathan and his brother were left to sort out Joe's affairs and they were in a nightmarish mess. Over the years, his record keeping had deteriorated to the point that there were only clues as to what he left behind. It looked as though he had tried to make things unnecessarily difficult for us, and why, I will never know. Trying to cope with our own life, sort out Joe's affairs, keep bosses and everyone else in our life happy was a juggling act for Jonathan and me for the next several months.

"At this point, the house project became a blessing for Jonathan in a way since he had to focus on it, and it was the distraction he needed to get through this time after Joe's death. People grieve for different things and for different reasons. I don't think Jonathan grieved for the loss of his father. I think he grieved for the loss of what could have been with his father. The could've, would've, should'ves of life are often the hardest to get beyond. I think Jonathan spent a good bit of time with these kinds of thoughts, although in the end, I know he did everything he could to foster a relationship with his father. I just don't think Joe had it in him.

"Autumn came that year, and with it, a brief respite of sorts. We had ultimately made our other deadline concerning the tax situation in late summer. We had finished the house except for some of the detail work, and we had been able to piece together enough details of Joe's life to do what had to be done to settle his estate. Just at the time we had begun to have hope that things were settling down some, Jonathan *lost his job.*

"No one was to blame really. As much as we wanted to be mad at his employer, we couldn't. The company he worked for was a statewide subsidiary of a bigger parent company who had many hundreds of employees. As part of a restructuring effort, most of the people in Jonathan's branch were eliminated regardless of merit or tenure. It was just part of the cost of doing business is the way we tried to look at it. When we took it down from that lofty plane however, what it translated into for us, and for Jonathan, was a tremendous loss, not only financially, but to Jonathan's self esteem as well.

"Coming on the close proximity of his father's rejection and death, this event started Jonathan on a downward spiral that made him start to retreat into himself. During this time, something broke inside him. I could see it happen before my eyes because I recognized it so well. I remembered the time something broke inside my soul and I had ever since been able to see when it happened in someone else.

"In many ways I suppose this time in our life was the beginning of the end of a lot of things for us. We had both been running on adrenaline for so long: the stress of waiting as long as we did to start building again, having to speed

things up as much as we did to get moved in, Jonathan's father dying so suddenly and the emotional toll it exacted, both of us working at outside jobs, having to mend fences with friends and family who felt somewhat neglected since we had to spend what precious little free time we had on the house project, trying to take care of everyday details of living, and then Jonathan's job loss -- all this created a very shaky emotional foundation for what was yet to come for both of us.

"Sometimes blessings come in disguises and as hard as it was emotionally on Jonathan, I think physically he needed these few months off from work. He used the time to look for work and catch up on all the unfinished details on the house. He was even able to relax some.

"To Jonathan, relaxing always meant fishing. I never knew anyone who loved it as much as he did. Try as I might when we were first married, I just couldn't work up any interest in it, so I was very relieved that his best friend, Eldon, loved to fish almost as much as he did. I was glad they had each other and this time together.

"In mid summer, Jonathan started working for a local company, doing for them what he had done for the other one -- except this job was local. With things back under control in our living situation, I was encouraged to think maybe life was getting back on track for us and we could look forward to some routine and regain some emotional strength. It wouldn't happen; less than a month after Jonathan started his new job, my father died.

"Though expected for a long time, it is always a shock when someone who has been a part of your life for so many years suddenly isn't. My father had had a bad heart attack almost twenty years before and had led somewhat of a limited life since then. Almost two years before he died, he had to have multiple-bypass surgery, from which I don't think he ever really recovered. On one occasion that he and my mother were visiting us between the time of his bypass surgery and subsequent pacemaker operation, and the time he died, I caught a glimpse of his broken soul -- the same type of defeat I had seen in myself once, and then Jonathan. By early autumn of 1991, I knew that coupled with his many physical infirmities, when I saw that look of loss in my father's eyes that he would not live long after that. He didn't, and I was glad his suffering had ended. I knew that part of my mother would die with him, and it did. Actually, he took almost all of her with him.

"Jonathan and I had now lost three of our four parents to death. I still had one grandparent living; he had none and had had none since before we were married. When I was a young woman, I had heard someone say that eventually we become our parents. I didn't understand what it meant at the time I heard it, but after my father died, I recalled hearing it again and realized I finally did understand. Though not parents ourselves, Jonathan and I were then both near or past the ages our parents were when we got married, and in that sense, we had taken their place in the scheme of things.

.   "I always spent much too much time in my life worrying about the future and being fearful of the 'what ifs'. I was fortunate I didn't have the crystal ball I wanted, into which we could look and get a glimpse of our future. If we could, there would be times in all of our lives that we would head for the nearest roof to jump off of. That was certainly true for the year and a half that followed my father's death.

        "As my sisters and I knew it would, his death took a toll on my mother's life and spirit that was irreparable by anything we said or did. She depended on him for more in her life than I have ever seen anyone depend on another person. It was as though her breath came through him. In time to come she would learn about the mechanics of life that she hadn't known about before, but she either couldn't, wouldn't or didn't want to get beyond a certain point of independence. *Chronic and acute illness visited her regularly in the intervening years and it was often the main topic of conversation during phone calls among her daughters. She refused to let go of anything material in her life which contained the slightest thread to her past and my father. She had always had great difficulty letting go of things, but following my father's death, I had this image of her going through life backwards physically, looking at and longing for her past, and having to be pulled into the future.*

"In many ways, she died the same day my father did, but by some twist of fate she kept breathing. Time stood still in her mind and the clock virtually stopped ticking that late summer day of his funeral. Forever after when I looked at or thought of her, all I could see was half a person, if that much. I knew if I looked close enough, I would see the look of total despair in her soul that I had seen before in my father, in Jonathan, and in myself. I knew what it felt like, and although she would have felt betrayed had I compared any kind of loss in my life with what she had endured, I knew what the pain felt like and it was hideous.

"We stayed a few days after my father's funeral in Virginia trying to help my mother get a grasp on some practical matters such as insurance, paying bills, etc. It was

a futile attempt, as I knew it would probably be, so we left her in my sisters' care and made the long trip back to our home to try to pick up the threads of our life once again. I knew no matter how long we stayed, we could not do the only thing that would have had any meaning to my mother, and that was to bring my father back from death. I often wondered why, during those last months of his life when he knew how gravely ill he was, my father didn't teach my mother more about finances and such. I suppose he either tried to no avail, or couldn't bring himself to deal with the reality of his situation. I guess none of us know how we would react unless faced with a similar fate.

"Losing one's parent brings a host of emotions to the surface to be dealt with. I was not overcome with grief or despair the way my mother was. In fact, for a number of weeks my sisters' and my mourning was held in abeyance while we tried to be a source of comfort for my mother. When I did take some private emotional time for myself, what I felt most was sadness for his suffering.

"Looking back over the years, I remembered how we never once discussed what happened in my teen years with Dean. It was like a family secret and was not to be brought up, although nearly every time I looked at either of them, I couldn't help but feel a sting or twinge of pain from that time. Perhaps it was for them as well whenever we had contact. I didn't invite that kind of recollection into my life. It was just there, ready to pounce with the right provocation. What happened all those years ago was an unresolvable issue. I knew they always felt it was Dean's fault and couldn't or wouldn't see the part of the pain that neither Dean nor I caused.

"A short three weeks after Jonathan and I came home, we bid farewell to another important person in our life, Richard Todd. Rick was young enough to almost be our son, and he and Jonathan and I had forged a unique friendship several years before. We had enjoyed his company so much at dinners, movies, yard sales, and day trips to tourist attractions. We had helped each other move several times, and we three could find humor in almost any situation we found ourselves in.

"His youthful outlook and upbeat attitude about life was a counterbalance to the cynicism that had started creeping into ours. His illness came during the time we had been in Virginia at my father's funeral and by the time we returned home, Rick had been diagnosed as terminal. We hardly had time to grasp the concept of it -- someone so young and full of life becoming so sick so fast -- when he was gone. We had promised to adopt his puppy Fritz (a miniature dachshund) 'if anything happened'. Since the 'anything' did happen, we had a tiny newcomer to our life who needed us much more than we needed him. That process soon reversed itself and he became the joy in our life and to everyone who came to our home. The other three dogs we had took him in like a long lost brother. He had his own bag of tricks for making people laugh, and was a constant source of amusement and pleasure. It seemed even the mischief he got into was a clever diversion on his part to lighten our heavy hearts.

"Two weeks after Rick's death, our emotional roller coaster took off again -- this time in an upswing -- when we had a two week visit from my British pen pal and her husband. She and I had been correspondents for 35 years, starting out as children, and had kept in touch all those years with letters, photographs, cards, and gifts. As remarkable as it now sounds, until Valerie called several months before to announce her trip, we had never talked on the phone or even heard each other's voices. It was truly a thrill of a lifetime when she and I met for the first time at the airport.

"Every minute of their visit was wonderful with the four

of us getting to know each other. It was a unique experience because we knew so much factually about each other, but having never met, it was somewhat like strangers becoming acquainted. It was wonderful seeing things around us through their lives. Every day was an adventure and learning experience about each other's environment. Each night after we cleared the table, we sat for hours over coffee exchanging ideas and asking and answering questions about each other's country, religion, politics -- nothing was 'off limits'. These discussions cemented a bond among us that I had not felt before in my life. When their all too brief visit was over and it was time to say farewell, we did so with tears all around but with a wealth of grand memories we could savor for years to come. As much as I wanted to accept their kind invitation for a reciprocal visit by Jonathan and me, somehow I just knew in my heart it wouldn't happen.

"My father's death, and then Rick's, were the first two in what would become a total of twelve deaths in our life during the next eighteen months. Some were family, some were friends, but all had an important place in our life. We didn't have time to adjust to one before another happened. Each person's passing took a little piece out of our souls, and toward the end of this sad time, I began to wonder just how

much was left. I felt numb inside and I knew Jonathan did too.

"In the midst of this mutual sorrow, Jonathan began experiencing some disturbing health symptoms. We both had been faithful about yearly checkups and pretty much followed doctors' advice. We also realized we were reaching middle age and had been through some extremely hard years emotionally and physically. We had not done all we could have to stay in the best of health, and perhaps we brought some of the strain on ourselves.

"Regardless, Jonathan's doctor suggested a very disturbing early prognosis of heart disease and wanted more tests. These tests and angioplasty revealed that while Jonathan did have a condition that needed monitoring, it was not as serious or life threatening as first thought. A lot of his prognosis was up to him, and he undertook a rigorous program of lifestyle modification that did wonders for him. In some ways, he became healthier, more fit, more informed, and more knowledgeable about his own body than almost everyone else around him, and he improved his odds significantly because of this. In this sense, he was ahead of the game because he knew what his limitations were and accommodated them in his life very well, whereas many people in his age group are walking time bombs without even knowing they have anything wrong.

"Along with other lifestyle changes to be made, Jonathan and I decided that we needed to streamline our surroundings, once again. This time, though, it would be different. We had stared fate in the face and had a reality check. The time was at hand to scale down everything in our life. We needed to do in our late '40s and early '50s what many people postpone doing until their mid-'60s, if at all. Our next move would be our last, and to a situation that either of us could maintain on our own.

"We became aware of how much of our life we had spent on things: working to have things; acquiring things; taking care of things; and finally, having yard sales at which we could dispose of things. It seemed comical when seen in that light. We took a realistic survey of all we had and were astonished to realize how much of what we had we could live without. We had done an about-face in our thinking: not only did we not need all we had; we no longer even wanted all these things in our life. We made a plan. We would move into a condominium about half the size of the house we were in, and we would take with us only that which we needed to really live. We knew this plan would hit hard with taxes, but it was a price we had decided to finally pay. Putting the plan to work was so much easier than I would have ever dreamed. It became our main focus. It became a cleansing and a liberating experience for us. We both felt our lives becoming freer.

"Most of the changes that were taking place were within ourselves. It seemed destiny was pushing us along a dark and mysterious road that neither of us had traveled before; yet somehow it seemed vaguely familiar to me. I pondered what transformations were taking place within me and Jonathan, puzzled by them, yet lured by the unseen grasp it had on me. I shared Jonathan's new awareness about life and its brevity. A new fatalism crept into my mind that influenced every thought I had.

"I knew something was working in our lives -- yes, 'lives', for somewhere along the way in the past five or more years, Jonathan and I had taken separate roads in life and much of our time was spent alone with ourselves; each going down different pathways, sometimes passing at intersections, sometimes visible only at a distance. I came to believe that what was working in our lives was a preparation of sorts, but for what, I had no idea, unless both our lives were coming to an end.

147

"Is this nature's preparation when someone's life is starting to wind down? Oddly, I wasn't scared by it. In some strange way, I started having a feeling of peace and serenity about life coming to an end. I shared some of my feelings with Jonathan, and he, too, was experiencing these same sensations. Neither of us knew what it meant, but neither of us were frightened by it either. Emotionally, Jonathan and I both had long ago shifted into neutral. Not many things brought us sadness anymore, but not many things brought us pleasure either.

"With no children and no siblings living near, it was up to us to take care of things and not leave a mess after we were gone. Having worked with lawyers so many years, I was very familiar with probate procedures. We wanted as little of that burden placed on each other or our families as possible.

"That same spring I received a letter about my upcoming high school reunion scheduled for Labor Day weekend in the fall. As time passed, I thought about it a lot. Not surprisingly, it brought back a lot of memories of those years and I began to actually feel some of the same sensations I had had then. Joy, happiness, terror, anger, hate, love -- all those things that seemed to be a part of that distant past. It was 1994 – could it actually be 30 years since we all left school that night and headed down different pathways?

"I had been to all the reunions since graduating, even making the trip from Florida once. Jonathan assumed I would want to go and was surprised when I told him of my reluctance. It really wasn't reluctance or disinterest. By then, we weighed almost everything we did by the amount of effort it took, and making all the arrangements to go would take a great deal of work. That spring I had had a traumatic health emergency that I was leery would repeat itself without warning while I was away. All of these things I kept telling myself and Jonathan, but I couldn't really explain why I simply didn't want to go. I wanted to want to go, but for some reason I didn't, and we left it at that.

" I knew in my heart I was not up to the emotional effort such an event demands. Waiting until the last minute to reply in case I changed my mind, I finally sent in my regrets along with a background summary sheet about myself since the last reunion. The weekend of the reunion itself I couldn't get it out of my mind. I started to call and talk to some of the people there, but didn't. I knew I would have to explain my absence and it was too complicated -- and too private -- to get into with anyone.

"My sister Veronica and her family were visiting us reunion weekend. Sidney had flown them down in his plane. When we took them back to the airport Sidney jokingly suggested he 'take me for a spin' in his plane before they left. All my life I had been kidded for having never even been in a plane. I was terrified of flying. I had no idea why, but I turned to Sidney and said 'Let's go'. Everyone froze in mid-sentence as Sidney and I boarded his plane and took off down the runway after what seemed like an eternity of checking things out, talking to the control tower and getting clearance to take off. I felt the exhilaration of speeding down the runway, and the ground dropping out from under me.

"I let out a squeal of delight as we climbed toward the clouds and I think Sidney thought I had had a heart attack. He kept asking if I was OK over the headphones. I know he could see my uncontrollable shiver since I was sitting in the co-pilot's seat next to him. The sensations were magnificent and such a contradiction of each other. I felt 'stark, white terror' and at the same time, I had an adrenalin rush I have never had in my life. I dared to look out the window next to me and saw the most exquisite patchwork quilt below. The land that I had driven over so much was now a huge vista of *fields and roads and tiny buildings. I don't know why, but I felt tears on my cheeks and when we landed, I had a welcome home committee waving and cheering and watching to see if I had to be carried from the plane.*

"Without knowing it, I had finally started to conquer fear of the unknown. In an instant, I had spread my wings and taken the first step back to life. Dean's call came a few weeks after that, and no one's life would be the same again.

"My life with Jonathan ended the next year when we divorced. In many ways, part of my life ended then as well. Jonathan left my life in 1995 and Dean entered it. The two worlds I lived in during that year could not have been more different."

"Micala, I had no idea that you could remember so much in such detail. I was pleased to hear so much emotion in what you wrote. Especially encouraging was the humor you interjected into the story of your move to Florida and the neighborhood crazies you encountered. I have long known that writing can be very therapeutic. It allows us to express emotions that we can't do in real life. It can be very cleansing. It helps to release the safety valve. It is also a gauge to me of an individual's ability to experience feelings even when they have withdrawn from the real world.

"In a way, I find it odd that there is very little anger in your story ... mostly sadness and a trail of tears. That is the depression speaking ... or writing.

"I have a good grasp of the issues we need to focus on, but instead of just hearing you say the words, I want to read your story this weekend. I will develop a multi stage plan for us to work from and we will begin when I see you again on Monday. In the meantime, keep up your meds, continue a limited routine and get a lot of rest. We have much work to do. It will be more intense than these two weeks have been and for that reason, I have set early morning appointments for Monday, Wednesday and Friday of next week. Depending on the progress we make, I might reduce it to Tuesday and Thursday later. We will take it as it comes. You don't realize it, but you have made a lot of progress from the woman I saw two weeks ago."

CHAPTER 33

Even though Dr. Blair had explained the EMDR therapy process to me, I was anxious as I entered his office.

The room was dark except for a small dim lamp behind me and in the shadows across the room I saw three other people there. Dr. Blair introduced them as doctors ... would I mind their being in the room as observers so they could confer about my diagnosis and observe the fairly new therapy he would be using. I almost laughed ... at this point, why were any of these formalities even necessary ... I was a goner anyway you looked at it.

Dr. Blair first explained the diagnosis ... as much for my benefit as the other doctors present. Clinical and circumstantial depression combined with Post Traumatic Stress Disorder and panic disorder. Combined, I had had a nervous breakdown.

"Dr. Blair, I thought only soldiers got PTSD."

"While it has gained attention in connection with combat veterans, anyone who has experienced trauma and suppressed it could fall victim to it."

So now the demon had a name ... several. I didn't understand all of it but he assured me in time I would be able to put the whole picture together. Good thing because if I had had a two piece puzzle to put together then, I couldn't have done it.

I only remember bits and pieces of it ... the repetitious eyework ... establishing pain levels ... resting ... going into my past to places he suggested ... establishing pain levels ... processing ... reprocessing. I wasn't remembering events ... I actually returned to them and when I did, I felt the emotions of that time and place ... crying, sobbing hysterically, vile guttural sounds I never knew I could make ... anger ... rage. He would stop this process, come back to the present and we would talk. This process was repeated several times that morning.

The next session, the one after that, and more than I can remember were much the same process with Dr. Blair. Same routine (minus the extra doctors) and Veronica drove me home. Life fell into a pattern ... keep my appointment with Dr. Blair ,,, and on my 'days off'' ... help Veronica do a few chores that needed to be done, and always plan some type of small outing for the afternoon ... mostly shopping at a store, a trip to the bank, a trip to the post office, going for a short ride in the beautiful horse country nearby, stopping to watch a frisky new colt rejoice in its new life, a walk across the street just to keep in touch with Carlo.

We always brought a bag of bread to feed the ever

hungry fish in the pond by Carlo's office. Sometimes we just fed the fish ... sometimes we just walked Fritz. Occasionally we would eat out or pick up take out or fix something simple to eat at home. Whatever it was and however our day was spent, it was kept as simple as possible, with no obligations or demands I had to meet, except to start taking care of myself again in my personal grooming. In a word, I had become a slob, not caring how I looked.

Veronica became the band leader, costume designer, set decorator, script writer and director for this artificial life I had come to live. It seemed unrehearsed to me, but had been very carefully orchestrated between her and Dr. Blair. The answering machine screened all my calls, Veronica answered the door and generally kept me behind a wall of protection which she could control.

CHAPTER 34

One part of the recovery process was to break my addiction and dependence on my computer. Instead of using it as a tool of pleasure, I had let it control my life. Another part of the process was to limit the contact I had with my gentlemen friends. I could let them be a part of my life on a limited basis. Of course Frank knew what was going on and I talked and emailed with him freely. The others I returned calls and emails to less frequently than before. 'My sister Veronica from Tennessee is visiting me' was a safe and honest reason I wouldn't be in touch or seeing them for awhile.

As the days wore on, the routine gradually changed as Veronica began to give me tasks to do ... load the dishwasher, run the vacuum, take care of the mail, take out the garbage. Our afternoon outings became more extensive ... a trip to the mall to shop, combining errands, etc. I started to drive again. All the while the therapy continued and I learned more and more about the depression and panic attacks that had plagued me for years.

The roots were in my childhood when my parents had expected so much of me and I was terrified of failure. I had compensated for this by trying even harder at whatever I was doing, becoming a perfectionist and starting to demand more of myself than they had. I could never reach the goals that either they or I set for myself.

My mother had been hospitalized with depression when I was 6 or 7 ... she had become paranoid that something would happen to me and Veronica and my father and she would be left alone. Because she held me so close, I too, became terrified of being alone. I also felt guilt that I had somehow failed her when she had to 'go away because she was sick'.

When Dean came into my young life, he wasn't part of their plan for me to succeed. They saw him as a stumbling block to my achievement. It was the first time in my life when my emotional side began to overrule my logic and I didn't know how to balance the two. When Dean first left my life all those years ago, I was traumatized by the feeling of loss, abandonment and rejection even though he had little to do with any of that.

I led my adult life in such a way as to shut down the emotional side and only deal with things intellectually. Business and success became my goals and I achieved a lot of what I set out to do. Jonathan's drive for the same things did not match mine, but he and I worked together very well to accomplish projects. It became a heady experience for me and the more I succeeded the more I wanted to. It was self reassurance that I was seeking and not fame or fortune. To me, happiness had no connection to the emotional side of life; only the logical, intellectual side.

I was forced to deal with emotions many times thru the years with illness or death of loved ones or one of my pets, which always sent me into a tailspin. I didn't have the equipment to handle it. It always left a deep scar on my heart and took me far longer in the grieving process than it did others.

The most traumatic of these times was when I came to the realization that my marriage was over ... about 5 years before it actually ended. Again, the embarrassment of failure, rejection and abandonment reared its ugly head and that was when my panic attacks began. For the most part I kept them from Jonathan. Occasionally he would catch me in one of them and I always feigned a flimsy excuse. I don't know that he ever believed me, but he would let it go at that.

We had tried marriage counseling for several months a year before Dean's sister made that fateful call and were mortified when the counselor confirmed my nagging suspicions that our marriage would probably not survive much longer (it did for 18 months more). Jonathan and I had become so wrapped up in the mechanics of life and achievement that somewhere along the way we lost the emotional side of our marriage. Bringing it out into the light of day by someone else confirming our suspicions made it all the harder to deal with the failure, rejection and abandonment issues I always did battle with.

We were experiencing emotional shutdown due to sensory overload. Simply put, it was too much to handle all at once. I remembered that same sensation from so long ago. Shutting down. Jonathan and I experienced our suffering privately ... within ourselves. We didn't rely on each other for help; I think instinctively we each knew the other had little reserve to share.

This pattern had been set in motion long before, but this sequence of events was the key that locked us emotionally away from each other for good. We both experienced loss differently and Jonathan and I relied only on ourselves for comfort and solace during this time.

Dean's second arrival in, and his departure from, my life forced me to deal with these same issues. It was doubly hard this time than when we were young. We were on our own now, and without intervention from anyone, we couldn't make it work. I blamed my parents for making me wait 30 years to find that out. I blamed myself for not having put an end to it when Dean first came back into my life and I began to see the red flags almost immediately. I blamed myself for not having the courage to admit making so many mistakes. I had succeeded very well in the intellectual side of life and had failed miserably in the emotional side.

While Dr. Blair was not certain if a specific event started my mental breakdown, he did know that each experience of failure, rejection, and abandonment only added to the weight of it throughout my life. Recently, each relationship I had, each man I met and fell 'in love with' after Jonathan, was doomed from the beginning. More weight to the pile.

The pile finally came crashing down when I could no longer contain life within that wall I had built around it and I started to run away from my demons ... the depression and PTSD ... and started making some very bad choices. I had a self destruct button that I couldn't stop pushing.

In time, I was able to recognize that I didn't have to hold someone so close to me to keep them from leaving my life. I learned that there was a big difference between needing someone and wanting someone; between loving someone and being in love with them.

I began to make the connection between logic and emotion and could finally see the pattern for myself. I was gradually able to unite thinking and feeling into a workable tool for decision making. Once you see the demon for what it really is, you know which weapons you need to fight it.

Fear stopped being my constant companion. I even started to like myself a little, warts and all, for the first time in my life. I began to forgive myself for not being perfect, and realized that I could let my frailties show without rejection. My feelings of hopelessness began to turn into small feelings of empowerment.

I slowly reclaimed enough of my life that I wanted to rebuild it. I wanted to go back to the work that I really loved ... law ... and restore some order to other parts of my life. I had a lot of catching up and owed a big debt to many people, most of which I would never be able to repay. I came to understand that some debts can't be repaid except to say 'thank you' or 'I am sorry' and let it go at that. Feelings of guilt can't repair or repay anything.

CHAPTER 35

Veronica's last day with me arrived and I was filled with anxiety, but a slight sense of relief. Her leaving was a signal that I was ready to ... needed to ... had to ... go back to life on my own. With her help ... no, it was far more than that ... she was a gift from God and a big part of my salvation. With God's help; with the help of a very capable psychiatrist; with the support and encouragement of a very few close friends ... and yes, with my own frail effort and determination to live and move ahead, it was time for me to see if I was up to the daunting task of living again.

I would continue to see Dr. Blair from time-to-time. After each EMDR session I always waited for the other shoe to drop but it never happened. Whatever issues we had reprocessed that day stayed reprocessed and I had long since ceased having the panic attacks.

I couldn't avoid problems; I would have to figure out how to handle them. I would have good days and bad days ... yes, I was afraid ... terrified that the bad days would begin another downward spiral into the depths of Hell from which I was just returning. I felt like a cancer patient whose cancer had gone into remission and wondered how long it would last. I wouldn't know until I was tested and the only way for that to happen was for Veronica to go back to her own life.

During the first days she was with me, she had been like a respirator ... forcing me to breathe when I didn't even want to. She has always had a keen sense of doing for people just what they needed at the time. She also operated on their timetable and not hers. There were times she would sit for hours and watch me stare out the window silently. When I cried, she was there with a shoulder. She kept track of the going to sleep, getting up, taking me where I had to go, kept the pill schedule, tended to Fritz and Tiger. When I napped, she went out for groceries or did other errands. She picked up mail, reminded me to shower or dress or change clothes or wash my hair. Depression, anxiety and PTSD are exhausting and it consumes what little emotional and physical energy one has. I couldn't do 'things' for myself so she did them. Whatever needed doing, she did in her quiet intuitive way. She truly had been my life support system and (months later) I learned that she had been able to strike a deal with my psychiatrist after my initial appointment to keep me from being hospitalized. She traded her life for mine as long as she needed to; on call and on duty 24/7. I could never repay her kindness ... I could just love her more than I already did.

The day was beautiful, a hot sunny summer blue-sky Florida day that I so loved. All too soon she was packed and

Crossing Bridges and Burning Others ... by Micala*

we sat down for another check list ... medication, pet needs, follow the schedule ... eating, sleeping, mail, reconnecting with friends, doctor appointments. She reminded me as she had a hundred times before that she could come back on a moment's notice or something close to that. I promised to remember that she was always going to be my safety net and knew in my heart that our roles of 'big sister, little sister' had been reversed forever. I knew that sharing the experience we had in the past weeks created a bond that would last a lifetime.

We had said all we needed to, all that could be said. The short drive to the train station was in silence ... we agreed we couldn't do this if either of us cried, so somehow we held it together. This short trip was a major leap of faith into the future for me and we both knew it. I helped check her bags and we found a comfortable seat to wait for the train. Why is it at a time like that, the train is always on schedule.

We stood, hugged until we squeezed the breath out of each other. Just as we felt each other start to tremble, I let go, smiled, kissed her and turned to walk back to my car. At the car door I turned back to see her looking at me from one of the train's windows. I forced myself to smile and wave ... she did the same and the train slowly pulled away.

I stood by the car until the train disappeared around that same corner I had once so anxiously watched for it to appear. That time it was coming south. This time is was going north. I got in the car, turned the key and began to slowly drive into my future. Were all the ghosts really gone? So much of my past life and so much of my recent life had been like an illusion. I thought I saw something that wasn't there once I got to it.

When I got back home I looked around I knew it was real, and Fritz and Tiger were real, and recent weeks had been real. With that knowledge, that was where I would begin again. This time I would bring with me only the most important, real things I needed. Would a male companion fit into my life again? What roll would Drew, Edward, Frank, Dean and Eric play, if any? Were they a part of my past or a part of my future?

The only way to answer these and all the other normal questions normal people have about what is to come is to take the next step that leads into tomorrow. First I had to deal with today, or what was left of it, by myself. I felt ready to do that. All the toys and all the traumas of my youth were put away now in a safe place. I finally had the adult tools I needed to live life. I would surrender to fate what I could not control and I would reclaim that which I could. With God's help, I would be able to distinguish between the two. A somewhat shortened and modified version of the Serenity Prayer, I thought to myself.

CHAPTER 36

I did a lot of introspective thinking after that. I had learned so much about myself and why certain things happened the way they did. Odd how so much of my life had been defined by imaginary dividing lines ... watershed moments ... before this and after that. The first big goal I set for myself was to stop seeing life in those segments. At any one of those crossroads, I could have taken the other path and life would have been different.

I needed new guidelines. Stop the 'what ifs' and S ... T ... O ... P thinking everything to death. It ... is ... what ... it ... is. Get on with life, because it is moving on whether I keep up or not. I could continue to sit and watch it pass, or get on the train.

At some point in my career years earlier, I felt burned out on law and decided to work at something entirely different. I signed up with a temp service and the first job assignment was working in a purchasing department for a large manufacturing plant which did mostly government contract work in the space industry. I ended up working 4 days a week for over a year at this place. I then left for two reasons: first, they wanted me to become a full time employee on the payroll (which I did not want to commit to), and two, I had a very nice offer of a part time job from one of the former law partners I worked for who had split off to form his own practice.

During that year, I loved learning the manufacturing process from beginning to end. It started with an order which was passed from department to department, thru engineers, research and development, to architects, builders, testing, telemetry, quality control, to shipping ... and finally out the back door or to the mail room. Some of the finished products would fit in an envelope to be mailed or sent by courier; others required a flat bed trailer covered in secretive tarp for transport.

Other than learning about the process of how something gets made, the most important thing I took away from that experience was a copy of a sign I saw hanging in the engineering department my first day at work. It said, 'there comes a point in the history of every project where you have to shoot the engineers and start production'. Not to be taken literally, of course ... but wasn't that one of life's biggest stumbling blocks? It certainly was one of mine.

Plan the work and work the plan. AND leave it at that no matter the outcome. AND move on. AND no looking back. It was time for me to do that very thing with life.